Heike Schuhmacher M.D.

VISION AND LEARNING

A Guide for Parents and Professionals

HOW UNDIAGNOSED VISION PROBLEMS CAUSE
LEARNING DIFFICULTIES AND WHAT YOU CAN DO
TO UNLOCK YOUR CHILD'S ACADEMIC POTENTIAL

Translated from German by Sabine H. Seiler, PhD
Illustrations and Layout
by Antje Schomacker, Art Director

© 2017 Heike Schuhmacher M. D.

Illustration, Design
Antje Schomacker, Art Director

Translator
Sabine H. Seiler, PhD

Original title
Fehler muss man sehen: LRS und visuelle Wahrnehmungsstörungen erkennen und behandeln. 2015 Tredition, Hamburg ©2015 Dr. med. Heike Schuhmacher

Editor
Tien Nhan Phan

ISBN
ISBN 13 : 978-1547007080
ISBN 10: 154700787

About the Author

Heike Schuhmacher, M.D., is a certified primary care and family physician, subspecializing in pediatric developmental disorders. Her private practice offers children with learning, perceptual, and concentration disorders comprehensive diagnosis of underlying neurophysiological and neuropsychological brain functions and an extensive range of individual therapies with emphasis on Optometric Vision Therapy.

Dr. Schuhmacher is certified as an Orthoptist by the German Ophthalmological Society. In her medical doctorate thesis conducted at Ruprecht Karls University in Heidelberg, she focused on the diagnosis and therapy of visual perceptual disorders in children diagnosed with dyslexia. Her research on this subject was based on a four-year collaboration between herself and Professor Kraus-Mackiw, head of the neuro-ophthalmology department at the university eye hospital with Heidelberg elementary schools and the university's child psychiatry hospital. Dr. Schuhmacher has worked as a consultant school physician for many years before establishing her own private practice. She continues to advise educators on perceptual aspects of specific learning disabilities, consults on Individualized Education Programs (IEP), and develops both design and implementation of special classroom accommodations for children with perceptual disabilities. Through her lectures and seminars, she contributes to the continuing education of educators, special needs teachers, therapists, pediatricians, child psychologists, and child psychiatrists.

Dr. Schuhmacher also specializes in developmental optometry and in 2010 was appointed Fellow of the American College of Optometrists in Vision Development (COVD), the first German physician to receive this honor.

More information about Dr. Schuhmacher and her practice can be found at: www.dr-schuhmacher.de and at the website for her book: www.fehlermussmansehen.de.

Table
of Contents

3 Neurophysiology of Vision

find out

Foreword
by Dr. Leonard Press

A book on any topic oriented toward parents and professionals is a very ambitious undertaking. After all, one of the cardinal rules of writing is that an author must first have in mind the audience that she or he is addressing. Given the substantially different levels of awareness that parents and professionals have about vision and learning, one has to admire the work of Heike Schuhmacher, M.D. in succeeding to find a solid and informative middle ground. The book that you hold in your hands, or that engages your eyes through the screen, breaks new ground for a wide readership.

Dr. Schuhmacher's success in this venture is no coincidence. I was first introduced to her seven years ago at the Annual Meeting of the College of Optometrists in Vision Development (COVD) and was immediately impressed by her passion and commitment to advancing her knowledge in the field. She had undergone the rigorous process of attaining Board Certification through Fellowship status, a remarkable achievement. At that time she shared her desire to write a book that would enlighten parents and professionals about the gap in transdisciplinary services she encountered in both the public and private sectors regarding vision based learning problems. The unique experiences that Dr. Schuhmacher brings to this venture therefore makes it a rich and unparalleled resource. Initially trained as an orthoptist with certification from the German Ophthalmological Society, Heike Schuhmacher obtained her M.D. while focusing on the visual perceptual disorders of children diagnosed with dyslexia.

There are additional blends of expertise that infuse this book with knowledge and experience. Having served as a consultant school physician before establishing her own private practice, Dr. Schuhmacher lends her insights to topics ranging from perceptual aspects of specific learning disabilities, to Individualized Education Programs (IEPs), to special classroom accommodations for children with perceptual disabilities. Assisted in her practice by a highly competent staff trained in both optics and developmental optometry, the book's contents reflects the international flavor and education of Dr. Schuhmacher and her team. I was thoroughly impressed with the German language version of the manuscript when Dr. Schuhmacher first shared it with me two years ago. Having taken a year of Scientific German in college, and through the richly illustrated graphics, a limited understanding of its message, but wasn't able to fully appreciate what a masterpiece Dr. Schuhmacher had written. The translation into English now reveals the breadth and depth of the material to me, and I trust it will to you as well.

The tone of the book is established in **chapter one**, allowing us to see the struggles of an underachieving child through his eyes, and the eyes of his parents. It briskly transitions into an appreciation of visual perceptual development in forming the building blocks of letter recognition and written language development. Visual memory and auditory memory are explained in simple to understand terms, serving as the basis for constructing a sight word and phonemic vocabulary that supports reading and writing systems.

Chapter two builds a bridge into the neuropsychology of vision in a way that makes it easy for both parents and professionals to appreciate the interconnectedness of the components of visual perceptual processing. It ranges from laterality and directionality to spatial orientation, and from visualization to visual intelligence, finishing with a flourish on the significance of primitive motor reflexes. The checklist at the end of the chapter on visual and motor skill deficits in pre-school-age children is the first of several useful checklists that can be found throughout the book.

Chapter three, the neurophysiology of vision, is a topic which could potentially cause parents' eyes to glaze over. But Dr. Schuhmacher handles this in a style that makes it very palatable to the layperson. The key again is allowing us to experience clinical issues through the eyes of Laura, a first grader already struggling to keep her head above the academic waters. However, there is no shortcut to the visual heavy lifting that the reader will have to do in the middle of the chapter to understand basic concepts in eye teaming, focusing and tracking and the pertinent neurophysiology of the visual pathways. Professionals, including vision specialists, will appreciate the extent to which the material is explicit and well organized. The subject matter comes full cycle when the story returns to Laura's struggles with eye teaming or fusion of binocular vision, and finishes with an enjoyable discussion about the benefit of 3D vision.

The material in the preceding chapters it put into a very useful clinical format in **chapter four** by asking a series of questions about the child's competencies in each of the skill areas related to the neuropsychology and neurophysiology of vision. There is a significant and well placed emphasis in this chapter on reading. But perhaps most importantly, we are introduced at the end of the chapter to a very useful construct in thinking about all these complex and interacting functions as piece of a puzzle. This allows us to conceive of the diagnostic process as a way of deciding which pieces of the puzzle appear to be missing, and how that can set the stage for effective intervention.

Chapter five addresses a set of complex issues which one does not normally encounter in books of this nature. As you read through the book I suspect you'll find at least one or two chapters after which you'll say to yourself: "It was worth buying the book for this chapter alone", and this chapter is no exception. There is much you will learn about the intricacies and relevance of Central Auditory Processing Disorders (CAPD). Most valuably, your eyes and ears will be opened to children who are plagued by deficits in both the auditory and visual realm. All too often when professionals or parents speak of multi-handicapped children, handicaps are considered in terms of severe impairment, and motor or cognitive systems are most heavily involved. This chapter places a spotlight on the more subtle issues of auditory and visual processing handicaps that can cooccur.

If you are a parent looking for the most useful chapter in this book, go straight to **chapter six**. The comprehensive checklists will organize your thinking and observations at the outset. But all professionals would do well to read this chapter thoroughly to gain a deeper appreciation of the issues that parents have to contend with. These include requesting accommodations in school, and optimizing the workspace for the child at home to cut down on the drama of homework. It is a well-elaborated version of recommendations for visual hygiene and visual optimization.

The **final chapter** assembles all of the puzzle pieces into a model for therapeutic intervention. The visually pleasing graphics in chapter seven will help you grasp a sampling of the options available for effective treatment of deficiencies and disorders identified in the preceding chapters. Neuroplasticity, motor- and neurofeedback, binocular awareness and attention, and brain changes in learning are addressed and best of all, you get to see how Mario and Laura utilize their newly acquired visual skills to shine in their educational environments.

I'll conclude by saying that as familiar as I am with much of the material in this book, I came away from reading it with a very uplifting feeling. If you are a professional, you will acquire a deeper appreciation for Dr. Schuhmacher's ability to connect the dots to form clear pictures. If you are a parent, you will be illuminated by the graphics and find light bulbs going off as the puzzle pieces interconnect for you.

Whether you read the book cover to cover, or cherry pick your favorite sections, you will learn how undiagnosed vision problems cause learning difficulties and what you can do to unlock the academic potential of children like Mario and Laura. There is no greater gift that you can give to a child, and I hope that you share this information with as many people as possible.

Leonard J. Press, O. D., FAAO, FCOVD
Optometric Director, The Vision & Learning Center
Fair Lawn, New Jersey, USA

Introduction

There is no problem with Mario's eyes; his eyesight is perfectly fine. But he is struggling with reading and writing and cannot keep up in school although the school psychologist has attested to Mario's normal intelligence. The cause of his learning disability lies in an undetected problem with visual functions and processing.

Such a disorder cannot be diagnosed by a brief routine check of visual acuity, but can seriously affect Mario's educational opportunities in general.

Many children are struggling like Mario. In fact, one in four American school children suffers from undetected perceptual problems. They may have difficulty focusing, or their brain may be unable to adequately process visual or auditory perceptions. But how can you tell whether your child is affected by such disorders? What causes them? And most important of all: What can you do to help your child?

School children with learning disabilities and concentration issues are frequently diagnosed with ADD or dyslexia, but many suffer from undetected disorders in perceptual brain functions and end up misunderstood and mislabeled. Even though your eye doctor (optometrist or ophthalmologist) attests to perfect eyesight, your child is struggling and failing already in elementary school when faced with tasks that require processing of visual information, tasks such as writing and reading simple words.

Many of these kids do not acquire the ability to use reading as a tool for learning. This deficit has a detrimental effect on their performance in all school subjects and limits their overall educational opportunities. In addition, these children develop spelling problems that have a devastating effect on their grades in both English and foreign language classes. Obviously, even perfect eyesight – 20/20 vision – is not enough. Neuroscience tells us 80 percent of our brain is dedicated to visual perception and processing. Our brain has six different centers for processing auditory perception and language but more than twenty different areas for processing visual information that enable us to identify and react to what we see – accurately and at lightning speed.

If your child has normal intelligence and a learning problem that is not remedied after a few weeks of practicing, practicing, and some more practicing, an in-depth analysis of these brain functions is absolutely essential.

THE GOOD NEWS

Once your child's disorder of visual functions and processing has been diagnosed, you can address the issue of what to do to help your child. Fortunately, visual functions respond very well to active treatment. The good news: Vision is an acquired brain function, and thanks to our brain's neuroplasticity, we can improve visual functions by learning. Children and even adults can learn how to train their eyes. With some training, children in elementary school can definitely improve their ability to concentrate, increase their speed in reading and comprehension, perceive and "scan in" spelling details already while reading, and develop the visual-spatial conceptual framework essential to mathematical thinking and excellent visual memory.

This Book

───────────────────────

→ **informs** parents, teachers, and therapists of children affected by disorders of visual functions and processing about the connections between vision and learning;

→ **describes** in a clear and understandable way what the neurophysiological processes underlying our visual functions are, what "processing of visual information" means, what this has to do with intelligence, concentration, and the ability to learn;

→ **explains** the role of visual perception in reading and writing and how certain forms of dyslexia are caused by disorders of perceptual brain functions;

→ **describes** the typical symptoms of disorders of visual functions and processing in school children;

→ **explains** how such disorders can be diagnosed;

→ **explains** how "Optometric Vision Therapy" works,

→ **provides** caregivers with advice on how they can assist children affected by visual problems.

───────────────────────

Help for Parents, Teachers & Therapists

If you are holding this book in your hands, you are probably a teacher or therapist who would like to gain greater insight into the nature of these disorders and the treatment options for children entrusted to your care so you can better help them.

Or perhaps you are a parent and suspect that your child has an undetected vision problem causing the struggle your child experiences. You want to better understand your child, and above all, you want to be able to help your child. In that case, the comments following below may be familiar to you.

"EVERY AFTERNOON I SPEND HOURS AND HOURS STUDYING."

→ CHILD *I often wonder what's wrong with me. Other kids do their homework quickly after school, study for tests, get A's and B's, and go play sports in the afternoons or play with their friends – why can't I?*

Every afternoon I spend hours and hours studying. Even when I try very hard, I'm glad if I get even a C- on my work. Often I get a D and a comment that I should try harder and study harder!!

My teacher often complains that my writing is so hard to read, or she scolds me because I cannot even copy anything from the blackboard without making mistakes.

Reading is so hard for me. Often, I don't understand the assignment and don't know what I'm supposed to do or what the question is in the first place. Often, I have to read an assignment two or three times before I understand what it is about, and then I don't have enough time left for answering the question even if I do know the answer.

"I CAN SEE THAT HE IS EXHAUSTED AND STRESSED WHEN HE COMES HOME FROM SCHOOL"

→ MOTHER He shows me his notebooks, and I see that letters end up above or below the lines and that the numbers are again halfway outside the little squares. His writing looks very sloppy, and I can tell that my son feels hurt by the teacher's comments for I know how long he has worked on his assignments and how much effort he has put into his homework.

Every afternoon we spend time doing homework together, which really takes hours and hours. Doing homework is stressful for both of us, and sometimes it's just a nightmare. Again and again, I find myself having to spur him on, having to be the one who forces her son do his homework. I can see that he is tired and how exhausting some homework assignments are for him. Of course, I would love to let him go play instead of laboring away at his homework. But if I let him do that, he would fall behind in school even more, and his grades would suffer.

So I just keep pushing him and endure his bad mood and the temper tantrums as calmly as I can, and every day I renew my efforts to work with him and help him out as much as I can. But I have to admit that I scold him too often and even yell at him sometimes and threaten to punish him, and I feel just awful doing that.

I often think that his siblings are definitely getting less attention because I need to spend so much time to help him with his homework. Luckily, the other kids have an easier time learning and don't need me as much. But that doesn't keep me from feeling guilty.

And then, when after all this work – really too much work – my little one goes off to school, full of hope for the next class test or essay, I start preparing myself for the moment, when he comes home and things went wrong again.

I suffer with my child, and after each of the many parent-teacher conferences in school, I go home with a heavy heart, make up my mind to support my son even more and more effectively. I often feel that I am responsible for his mistakes, and my husband and the grandparents also blame me. They often say that the boy just needs to work harder and make more of an effort and that I have to do a better job of helping him.

I keep hearing people talk about concentration disorders! I don't understand why concentrating on his school work is so difficult for my child even though he doesn't have this problem all the time or in every case. Why does my son have such great difficulties concentrating on writing, arithmetic, or doing his worksheets and doing them correctly? And why is reading especially difficult for him?

He is a very good listener. When I read to him, he understands immediately what the text is about and remembers every detail. He would love it if all his books could be audiobooks. In his general studies class he is often one of the most engaged students. He is interested in so many things. When I've read to him at home what he needs to know, he remembers what I've read, has lots of questions, and is clearly excited and eager to learn more.

Are there concentration disorders that occur only in connection with certain activities? And if so, is that really ADHD?

"I AM VERY WORRIED ABOUT MY CHILD'S FUTURE"

→ FATHER *Sometimes I dread coming home after work, because I know the scene awaiting me there: My wife and my child are totally exhausted again but are still not finished with his homework. Both will be in a bad mood, and once again tempers will have flared, and they'll have had a quarrel. When I see my child's poor performance and see that the latest test turned out badly again even though my wife and child say they studied hard for it and prepared diligently – well, I can't help wondering what they're doing all afternoon.*

I know that my child is not stupid. I know that my wife is desperate and makes every effort to supervise our child's learning closely and that, of course, she loves our child more than anything else in the world. But when I look at the results of their efforts, I cannot help asking: "What is going on here?"

When I study with my child on weekends, we are both perhaps a bit more relaxed then, but I also experience the things my wife tells me about. I have to accept that I cannot really help my child either. I am very worried about my child's future and must admit, "I'm at a loss and don't know what to do next."

"I KEEP LEAVING WORDS OUT WHEN I READ"

→ CHILD *In my remedial class I often have to do exercises to improve my handwriting, and I'm embarrassed that I can't do a better job. My teacher keeps telling me: "Write another 0, concentrate more when you practice your next curves, then you will eventually develop nice handwriting." I try hard, but nothing changes.*

When I read, I keep leaving words out or getting the word endings mixed up. Sometimes I read words that aren't even there, and then the text seems so strange to me that I cannot understand anything. I hate reading! When I have to read aloud, I always feel sick because I already know that I cannot do it right, and I'm afraid the other kids will laugh at me.

It takes me so long to write one page, and then what I've written is full of mistakes. Most of the time I try to write only very short essays because it takes me forever to correct all my mistakes. And I can never find all of them by myself. I just don't notice when a word is is misspelled: My parents always say that I'm just not paying attention and don't concentrate; they say if I'd only look carefully, I'd see what I misspelled again, for the hundredth time, even though yesterday I still could spell it correctly.

I've told my parents that my eyes hurt when I read and that sometimes the letters are a bit wobbly and sometimes I can't clearly recognize them. I often have headaches after school and when I'm doing my homework.

Mom took me to the eye doctor right away because we thought that maybe I'd have to wear glasses. I'd have worn glasses even though I think they're ugly. But the eye doctor said I have eyes like a hawk and can see even the tiniest letters just fine!

And now my parents think I'm just looking for an excuse to get out of having to do my homework. So I'm simply not saying anything about this anymore. I know I'm not lazy or stupid, but sometimes I think that perhaps that is what I am after all because I simply cannot get my homework done the way I want to.

If you know a child who is saying things like that, or if you can put yourself in the shoes of the parents above because you're dealing with the same situation, then you already know that undetected disorders of visual functions and processing can severely affect not only the child but the entire family.

Many parents feel guilty and wonder what they've done wrong in the upbringing and teaching of their child. In the worst case, they blame each other or believe the school or the teachers have caused their child's problems.

HOWEVER, THERE IS GOOD NEWS – VERY GOOD NEWS, IN FACT. AFTER READING THIS BOOK, YOU WILL BE FIRMLY CONVINCED THAT NEITHER YOU NOR YOUR CHILD NOR YOUR CHILD'S TEACHERS ARE TO BLAME FOR THE PROBLEM. INSTEAD, THE CHILD'S DIFFICULTIES ARE THE RESULT OF A MEDICAL CONDITION THAT CAN BE DIAGNOSED PRECISELY AND TREATED SUCCESSFULLY.

For the most part, the causes for developmental disorders are unknown

As with other disorders of child development, we do not know exactly **why** these functional and developmental disorders of visual functions and processing occur. As of yet, we do not even know exactly why some people develop nearsightedness and others do not. Many scientific questions regarding vision have still not been answered conclusively.

In any case, the answer to the question "why" would not help your struggling child. What would really help is clarification of the problem, the details surrounding it and finding means for overcoming this barrier for learning.

Vision is the basis for successful learning. Seeing well is not something we are born with; it is a brain function that develops through learning. In other words, we can learn to see better at any time and to make better use of our visual functions.

Perhaps with this book you're embarking on a somewhat challenging journey as the functions of the visual system are very complex. But reading this book will help you understand how vision and visual processing works. You can read the book consecutively, from beginning to end, or select only a few chapters that are especially interesting for you at this time.

KEEP IN MIND

You are by no means alone with this problem. Countless parents are also wondering why their child has such learning difficulties. Several years ago, the American Parent Teacher Association (PTA) pointed out in a published statement that an estimated 10 million American school children are suffering from undetected visual problems and urgently need help as they lag behind in school and fail to fulfill their potential.

In many English-speaking countries, unlike in Germany, it is fairly easy to find help because there are many specialized pediatric optometrists trained in diagnosing and treating such disorders. Their field of expertise is called **"Developmental Optometry,"** and in this book you will find a wealth of information about this area of pediatric optometry.

1

Chapter

Vision and Learning

VISION
AND LEARNING

1.01
READY FOR SCHOOL?

Starting school is an important experience for all kids. Most kids are excited about making new friends, learning new things, and finally doing everything the "big kids" can do. Surveys of kids in the first week of school usually find that 98 percent of children starting school are enthusiastic, highly motivated, and eager to learn. Only 2 percent feel uneasy or reluctant about going to school, usually because their time in preschool has not been a good experience or because they have seen older siblings struggle with homework and learning.

Six months later, the same survey yields a startlingly different result: only 50 percent of children answer with a wholehearted "yes" that they like school; 30 percent are neutral, and 20 percent have already lost the joy of learning and no longer like going to school.

To be successful in learning we need a combination of motivation and ability. When effort and work do **not** yield recognizable positive results, we inevitably become frustrated. This applies to children and adults equally. The human brain works best with a mixture of curiosity and positive emotions. We all love to succeed in our endeavors. When first graders no longer enjoy learning after only six months in school, it's surely not because they lack motivation. Rather, early and repeated experiences of failure, frustration, and self-doubt bring even the most motivated children to the verge of despair.

SUCCESSFUL LEARNING = MOTIVATION & ABILITY

How do you like school?

first week of school

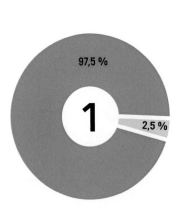

How do you like school?

second half of school year

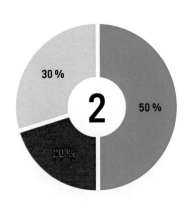

For Some Children Learning Is No Longer Fun

The reasons for this loss of enjoyment and self-confidence vary widely, of course, but with 20 percent of disaffected children we are dealing with a large number of children struggling in school and burdened with failure already in first grade. Interestingly, international statistics about physical exams of first graders published annually by health departments show that about the same percentage of children have developmental deficits in the areas of speech development and fine motor skills. Since it is very important for school children to hear and see well, their hearing and vision are usually tested before they start start school. Unfortunately most are screened only for visual and auditory acuity.

In most cases, children are tested with pure tone audiometry, which is an important method using sinusoidal tones generated at known frequencies to determine whether a child is hard of hearing. However, like many other screenings, this test does not address the complex functions of auditory perception and language processing.

Vision screening checks the acuity of each eye at a distance of 20 feet but does not assess more complex visual functions. When no problems are found from hearing and vision screenings, doctors, parents, and teachers assume that the child can see and hear well. When that child later develops learning difficulties, no one suspects that these problems have to do with vision or hearing.

However, not considering that connection is a serious mistake. To be successful in learning to read, write, and do arithmetic, children need information processing functions that require more than good visual acuity in each eye and normal hearing test results. **For children, school poses the challenge of an audiovisual high-performance system** that requires complex hearing, speech, and visual functions. Unfortunately, many parents and teachers are not aware of this.

As studies show, pediatric preventive checkups notwithstanding, one out of five or 20% of first graders start school with developmental deficits that can have a negative impact on the child's readiness for school and learning. Unfortunately, there are no definite findings yet on how many of these first graders also suffer from undetected visual or auditory processing disorders simply because these disorders are not discovered by routine checks.

MY WISHES ...   LAURA, SECOND GRADE

AL mi wishes

My nam is Laura
Ant im f jaers olb
I woht to b a beter
riter.

Ant reed Lke my
frengs.

1.02
WHAT IS DYSLEXIA?

The first scientific descriptions of people with reading problems date back to the late nineteenth century. In 1896 the British physician Pringle Morgan in an essay described the problem and called it "reading blindness." He also coined the term **"dyslexia,"** which is composed of the Greek term **dys** (prefix denoting bad / difficult) and **lexis** (suffix denoting words / language).

About one hundred years ago, in 1916, the Hungarian psychiatrist Pál Ranschburg described his patients' problems in learning to read and write as "reading and writing disability." This disability, for which Morgan's term **dyslexia** has survived and now is the generally accepted designation, can affect children even though they attend school regularly, work hard, and have no intelligence deficits.

The World Health Organization's (WHO) current diagnostics criteria list "reading and writing disability" among psychological disorders as a so-called **specific learning disability**. The achievements of children with this disability are considerably below those of their peers despite similar intelligence levels. Children having difficulties reading and writing are diagnosed with dyslexia only if those difficulties are not due to vision or hearing impairments. The WHO classification does not include the visual and auditory processing disorders discussed, but refers to patients with a disability in reading and writing despite normal eyesight and normal hearing.

Dyslexia, the specific learning disability in reading and writing, affects children all over the world, regardless of what their language is. The disorder is about equally prevalent globally, but affects about three or four times more boys than girls. According to estimates in England, about 15 percent of all school children suffer from some form of dyslexia; and statistics indicate that in the United States about 15 to 20 percent of school children are also affected. About 60 percent of these children have a close relative who is also suffering from dyslexia, which suggests that genetic components play a role in how the disorder develops. Scientists all around the world are working hard to identify the causes of this disorder, which first manifests in childhood but can often lead to difficulties and impairments that last throughout life. In their research, scientists have come up with countless models and theories regarding the origin and treatment of dyslexia, and most now focus on the disorder's linguistic aspects.

In the following chapters you will learn that the cause of some forms of this specific learning disability can be diagnosed medically. Reading and writing are based on visual, auditory, and language information processing, and deficits in these fundamental brain functions cause learning disabilities such as dyslexia. In the next section, you will be introduced to Mario as he moves from preschool to first grade. From the story of his struggles, you will learn more about the symptoms and behaviors children with an undetected disorder of visual perception and processing can develop as they start school.

1.03

MARIO IN FIRST GRADE: STARTING SCHOOL WITH UNDIAGNOSED DISORDERS OF VISUAL PERCEPTION AND PROCESSING

Mario is the youngest of three siblings and is very glad to start school at last. He has been looking forward to this for a long time and wants to learn and do all the things his older siblings can do. However, his mother was somewhat concerned because, unlike her other children, Mario does not show any interest in letters and numbers, does not like to paint, and does not want to sit with the older kids when they are doing their homework. She noticed that though Mario can spell his name, he sometimes inverts it, writing it from back to front, and other times he only twists the letter R around.

In preschool, Mario was a cheerful and creative child full of wonderful ideas for games to play. He often used free time to play outdoors. On rainy days, he could usually be found in the corner with building blocks. His pediatric check-ups showed him to be normal in all tested spectrums, but in his first days at school, teachers noticed that he held the pencil awkwardly and had trouble tracing shapes correctly. For example, Mario's rectangles did not have sharp corners, and his triangles looked like lopsided circles. When he was asked to connect dots with lines and to reproduce a given picture or pattern, Mario was unable to do it. His first weeks in school soon turned out to be a nightmare.

Mario's teacher was strict and corrected every one of his scrawled letters – with a red pen, of course – and she always had to remind him of his tasks because as soon as she was no longer standing next to him, he would stop working, get up and walk around and interrupt his classmates. Mario had great

HE KEPT CONFUSING 9 AND 6.

difficulty remembering the names of the letters of the alphabet and claimed "they all look alike anyway." When he was learning to write numbers, he kept confusing 9 and 6. When Mario had to count dots or pictures in order to learn the correct number symbol to assign to them, his count was often wrong.

When Mario copied words from the blackboard or a book into his notebook, his writing was riddled with errors. He often left out letters or even entire words. When teachers pointed out the mistakes, Mario would get angry; he seemed unable to see and recognize the mistakes. For a simple word dictation exercise, Mario's mother had to practice with him for hours. Even so, he would make mistakes, and always new and different ones as well. When Mario was not sure how to spell a word, he would spell it phonetically. That is, he would say the word out loud to himself and write it down as he heard it. Even after much practicing, he still could not remember what the words looked like.

Mario's parents and teachers noticed that the boy tended to give up quickly, to avoid his homework whenever possible, and to be tense with effort regardless how simple the task. The radiant and cheerful preschooler had turned into an unhappy boy who said he wanted to "quit school." The afternoons of doing homework were getting more and more unpleasant each time.

Mario's mother became alarmed because he was not learning to read the way his older siblings had. It was only with great effort that he could identify the individual letters, but then he could not re-integrate them into a whole word. When she helped him to integrate letters into a word and read it, even one consisting of only four letters, he was unable to recognize that same word when he saw it again in the next line. And so the whole laborious process of analyzing the word had to be started all over again.

Mario's learning problems

→ **Difficulties using a pen to** trace lines, color shapes, and draw pictures

→ **Difficulties** processing and correctly reproducing the visual features of numbers and letters

→ **Difficulties** remembering which letter represents which sound (phoneme-grapheme correspondence)

→ **Difficulties** combining sounds into a word, recognizing letter combinations, memorizing them, and reproducing them correctly.

Mario's mother then talked to his teacher, who expressed concern about Mario's problems with concentrating on his work and his disruptive behavior in the classroom. For the teacher, these two issues were the main reasons for Mario's learning difficulties. Her suggested solution for Mario's problems with writing and reading: practice, practice, and practice some more. She reassured Mario's mother that "some children just need a little more time to learn."

As a precaution, Mario's parents took the boy to two pediatric ophthalmologists because they feared he had a vision problem. Both ophthalmologists told them Mario has "eagle eyes" and that his problems were in no way connected with his eyesight.

Neither Mario's parents nor his teachers had ever heard of visual functions other than visual acuity, and they had no idea that these other functions are crucial for successful learning. Thus, they did not suspect that Mario was suffering from an undiagnosed disorder of visual function and processing.

1.04
FROM SPEECH TO WRITING

Nowadays we expect children to learn to read and write in about one school year. All around the world children in first grade learn letters or other abstract written symbols to turn spoken language into writing that can then be read. Still, the right to education and the view that all human beings should have the opportunity to learn to read and write have gained currency relatively recently in human history. For example, in Germany compulsory education was introduced about 300 years ago, and it's only since then that the opportunity to learn reading and writing has been available for all children.

The route from the development of human language to the first graphical symbols carved into stone and then to compulsory education in reading and writing for all has been very long. Language developed over a very long time, a process now generally assumed to have begun about 500,000 years ago with sounds and gestures. It took about 200,000 years before a complex language emerged. Hand in hand with the development of language, people's desire to express themselves in pictures grew, and in ancient cave paintings created more than 40,000 years ago we can see not only pictures of animals and humans but also symbolic lines reminiscent of writing symbols.

The development of symbols that could make spoken language visible began about 5,000 years ago. Writing came to be used as an aid in memory and as a means of communication and the exchange of ideas. Writing preserves the contents of spoken language beyond the moment of speaking, and this content can come alive again at any time when the writing is read. Clearly, the invention of writing is one of the most impressive achievements of humanity.

For example, in ancient Egypt, the ability to represent spoken language in symbols was considered magic, both terrifying and awe-inspiring, and was reserved for priests only. Their writing mistakes were even punishable by death.

The Egyptian word for writing was the same as that for drawing and means "drawing a line." Originally, writing consisted of a sequence of pictures like those found in Egyptian tomb paintings. Similarly, Chinese writing is based on ideographs, that is, symbols depicting concepts. These ideographs are still in use today, though in somewhat modified form. Through the vast Chinese empire with its many different languages and dialects such a writing system ensured that, independent of pronunciation, every reader could **see** what is meant. However, such writing systems present an enormous challenge for our visual and language memory because the symbol for each word must be memorized. Chinese school children must learn up to 3,000 characters just to be able to read basic books.

The **alphabet**, the so-called **phonetic writing** of ancient Greece, presents a very different way to "translate" spoken language into visible symbols. Using a phonetic writing system requires a rather advanced capacity for abstraction, for here there is no picture related to the concept but only graphic forms, called graphemes that represent individual speech sounds. The look and shape of these graphemes is not in any way related to the sound represented. An abstract code consisting of lines, curves, and dots that can be combined in any number of ways represents the great variety of spoken language. In this graphical code, the letters can represent the sounds of any language. We can read the letters and pronounce them when we know the pronunciation rules of a language – that is, when we know which grapheme corresponds to which sound or phoneme.

COMPONENT PARTS OF ALPHABET LETTERS

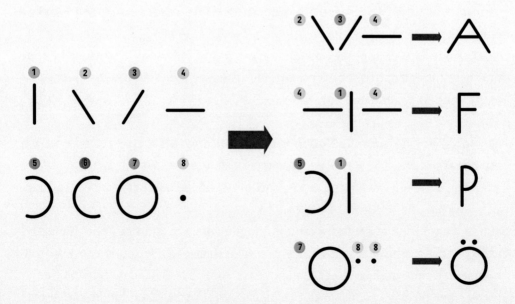

1.05
LANGUAGE ANALYSIS IN FIRST GRADE: DECODING WORDS

By the time children learn writing and reading, they must have reached a level of language development that allows them to analyze language as they hear and speak it. This means that in addition to experiencing language as a means of communication, they must develop an awareness of its structure. In particular, children must be able to understand that language has units smaller than words and that words can be segmented into syllables, sounds (phonemes), initial sounds, and final sounds. This process is called phonological analysis, and it involves questions such as the following:

> **DOES G SOUND DIFFERENT FROM K ? HOW IS THE PHONEME M DIFFERENT FROM N, AND HOW CLEARLY CAN I HEAR THE DIFFERENCE IN SOUND? WHEN I SAY A WORD, DO I KNOW WHAT SOUND THE WORD BEGINS WITH? AND WHAT SOUND IS AT THE END OF THAT WORD? AND WHICH WORD IS LONGER: MINUSCULE OR BIG?**

Such questions can be answered only if we can examine words structurally, independent of their meaning. Analyzing spoken language phonologically requires a considerable capacity for abstraction. After all, children must learn to use a writing system that dissects spoken language into its smallest functional units and represents these symbolically. These smallest units, the vowels and consonants, are not natural but artificial segments, in the sense that we do not pronounce words one letter at a time. After all, babies trying out language with their babbling do not produce pure individual sounds and certainly not pure consonants such as **K** or **D**.

In fact, the infant's very first speech sounds originate from accidental muscle movements in mouth, throat, and larynx and sound like **brra, krra, arree**. The smallest natural unit of language is the syllable, usually a vowel and consonant combination; infants explore syllables during the so-called babbling stage of speech development by endlessly repeating **mamama, bababa, gugugu** with some variations. Through constant communication and praise, babies learn which repetitions of which syllables make sense. **Mama, papa, wow-wow, mye mye** – the so-called protowords develop at this stage. At a somewhat later stage, babies utter their first combinations of syllables, such as **bye-bye, teddy**.

The knowledge that our spoken language has two kinds of qualitatively different sounds, vowels and consonants, that can be combined in many different ways, is not innate but learned. That words begin with a particular sound and have an ending sound is also something we are not usually aware of when we speak.

For many children the learning process of segmenting the continuous flow of speech and isolating particular sounds is initially very foreign. After all, in natural spoken language individual words are not isolated the way they are in writing. Instead, they slide into each other as in "thischear" for "this year." Asking first graders how many words are in the sentence: **"A dog is coming around the corner"** usually elicits the correct answer of seven, but when spoken aloud at conversation speed, the sentence sounds like it has only two words: **Adogiscoming** and **aroundthecorner.**

Saying individual words by themselves actually makes them sound a bit unnatural, not at all like natural speech that comes alive for us through little breathing pauses, voice modulation, and emphasis.

DOES G SOUND DIFFERENT FROM K?
HOW IS THE PHONEME M DIFFERENT FROM N
WHICH WORD IS LONGER:
"MINUSCULE" OR "BIG"?

Analyzing language into its phonetic components and then assigning these to graphical symbols requires a considerable capacity for abstraction from our sensory experience of speaking and hearing language. Children who have even minor residual symptoms of a developmental hearing or speech disorder – one thought to have already been overcome – are bound to have serious problems with learning to write and read.

1.06
LEARNING THE LETTERS OF THE ALPHABET: VISUAL COMPONENTS

The first step in learning to read and write is learning the alphabet, that is the so-called phoneme-grapheme correspondence in which phonemes get associated with the abstract symbols representing them. For example, two slanted lines with a crossbar are designated as **A**; three lines, one of them vertical and the other two horizontal, symbolize **F**, a consonant with specific rules for pronunciation. When another horizontal line is added, we have the vowel **E** which has its own phonetic characteristics, quite different from those of the other letters. A line with two arches is called **m**, and a line with one arch is an **n** which represents a very different sound from the other letter.

The letters **b** and **d** are especially useful examples for showing that perception and recognition of spatial relationships and spatial orientation of graphic symbols is an indispensable basis for learning the letters of the alphabet and thus for learning to read and write. Children who have problems in this area will continue to stumble when reading. Mistakes will be made when they cannot correctly associate each phoneme with its abstract symbol in a matter of milliseconds.

Spatial Perception and Orientation

Correctly and reliably identifying the position of graphical symbols in space requires an abstraction that actually goes against children's prior experience of the world. Toddlers learn that objects remain the same even when seen from different angles: Mummy seen from the front or in profile is still definitely Mummy. A chair remains a chair whether seen from the right or the left side.

To some extent, this experience of object constancy, which gives children a sense of security and stability, now must be given up in order to distinguish between the letters **b** and **d, p** and **g** or **q, w** and **m** as well as **a** and **e** or the number symbols **6** and **9**.

Mario is looking forwarb going to school because here he will finally learn to reab and write. You neeb to know a lot of letters, to reab all the wonberful dooks they have in the lidrary.

Moreover, unlike in English, in some languages when reading numbers with two or more digits, the digit on the right is spoken first before the one on the left – that is, speaking proceeds opposite to the usual left-to-right orientation of writing and reading. Learning one of those languages thus can be especially challenging for children with difficulties in spatial perception and orientation.

Form Constancy

Form constancy refers to the visual ability to abstract principles of graphical presentation and to identify and recognize them even when they appear in slightly modified form. For example, we are using many different typefaces, and for first graders it is quite an achievement to recognize the basic shape of the letter A in all these variations. Many elementary schools introduce block letters, both in capitals and lowercase in first grade and even want to teach cursive writing as soon as possible. For children with relatively minor deficits in visual perceptual processing this approach can be too much to handle and cause great learning problems already in the first few months of school.

For some children the transition from writing block letters to cursive writing is particularly difficult because they have to transfer their laboriously acquired ability to recognize shapes and correctly associate phonemes to graphemes – an ability of a fairly high level of abstraction – to writing symbols that look very different even though they have the same name and function. When reading texts in the very clearly structured typefaces Arial and Times New Roman, some children easily confuse the vowel symbols **e** and **a**.

d is now *d*   **l** is now *ʃ*   **L** is now *L*

Even in their books, children encounter many different fonts, all of which represent the same phonemes. However, children for whom perceiving form constancy is difficult, will find this very confusing.

Figure-Ground Perception

To identify and recognize shapes confidently and at great speed even when the background is very varied we must have functioning figure-ground perception. School children with deficits in figure-ground perception find it difficult to place abstract shapes, such as letters and numbers, on quad-ruled paper or paper with many lines.

For instance, paper with triple lines is designed to help first graders learn to write by helping them correctly place the descenders and ascenders of cursive letters. However, for children with difficulties in figure-ground perception these lines can flicker and make **letters difficult to recognize against the background of the flickering lines**; so they feel tired and exhausted after writing only a few words.

Children with these issues realize that their classmates have no problem at all with these simple tasks, and their frustration with their own efforts grows. Of course, they are not able to tell their parents or teachers what their difficulty is, that they are suffering from problems with figure-ground perception. To find out what the problem is, adults must observe closely how the child works and avoid attributing all learning problems to a lack of concentration.

1.07
GONE IN SECONDS: AUDITORY WORKING MEMORY

Memory is the ability to store information, organize it, and retrieve it as needed. This process can be quite deliberate, for example, when we are learning something new and want to remember it. We distinguish between long-term memory, which has a huge storage capacity, enough to hold many decades' worth of memories, and short-term memory, which stores information for a few minutes only. In addition, our working memory stores information for only about **45 to 60 seconds**. It functions as a kind of buffer memory or intermediate storage area, storing information just long enough and **in the order it was received** – that is, sequentially – until it can be processed further elsewhere in the brain or can be deleted if it turns out to be irrelevant.

When we are learning, working memory obviously plays an important role, and this is especially true of the so-called auditory working memory. This function allows us to briefly and sequentially store information heard, spoken, or thought. With this memory function, we can understand the linguistic contexts because we can remember what has been said just a moment before and so understand the meaning of a sequence of words. Ultimately, this memory function allows us to store spoken information long enough to be able to analyze it.

Without such a memory function, the spoken word is ephemeral, as you have perhaps found out for yourself when listening to an interesting talk or lecture or a boring class in school. In both cases someone is talking for a long time and saying many things that might interest you. But even if you listened attentively, a short time after the event you can remember only a few details – unless you have taken notes.

Writing, one of the most brilliant inventions ever, serves us as a memory aid: when we use a smartphone, a computer, or paper files. If you want to remember appointments, write a shopping list, or capture an idea, you use writing as a "preservative." Of course, when we store memories not in the brain but in an external storage medium, there can be mishaps, such as writing a letter or important text on the computer or other device but forgetting to save it – and then suddenly it's lost and "gone."

Spoken language is just "hot air" – literally. In speaking, we generate vibrations in the air that reach the ear of the listener and there causes the ossicular chain in the middle ear to vibrate. Via the auditory nerve's processing systems these vibrations then activate the brain regions that deal with the perception and understanding of language.

These vibrations of air are at the core of spoken communication, and they are incredibly fast. But as soon as we stop speaking the entire flow of language vanishes into thin air, literally. Information that is transported at high speed via air vibrations is a purely temporal, ephemeral event. For example when we spell out a word. This information can be preserved for the long term through a system of visual symbols, such as writing, which children begin to learn when they first attempt to trace shapes and letters in first grade.

Children Need Auditory Working Memory to Transfer Words into a Phonetic Writing System

We can learn to write in a phonetic writing system only if we can analyze the spoken language phonologically and transfer it into a visual recording system that represents the sounds as letters on the page. Clearly, this requires perfect speaking and hearing. To spell words we need a good auditory working memory to temporarily store the speech sounds and letters during the spelling process until that process is completed.

This working memory is the simplest phase in our memory storing process. New information is stored in the sequence in which it is received, chronologically until this information can be processed further. Our working memory forms the central "scaffolding" for understanding language. For example, someone says first this and then that and then this other thing, and usually, we understand what that person wants to convey holistically after we have heard several consecutive words or sentences. We listen to another's words and briefly store those words in our working memory until we have grasped the meaning and can move on to the next level of understanding. In the moment we do that, what is stored in the working memory is automatically deleted to make room for new spoken information.

This brain function works within a very small window of time of only a few seconds, and after that time the information stored is deleted, whether it is processed further or not, to make the working memory available again. The working memory's essential function is thus to keep available information as it arrives sequentially, one item after the other. The working memory temporarily stores information whose meaning we have not yet grasped until complex regions of language comprehension in our brain can establish connections and transfer the information to a higher level of processing. For example, our working memory enables us to understand a story by storing information that answers these questions:

→ **Who** did what when and where?

→ **What** are the names of the people doing things?

→ **What** did they experience?

→ **Where did the** actions take place?

→ **When** did the protagonists experience a certain event?

It is only thanks to this ability – of remembering details and imagining something in detail – that we can create a **"movie in the mind"**. This is what makes listening to a story or reading one ourselves so enjoyable.

Children exercise this ability early on. For example, they want to hear a favorite story repeated again and again, hundreds of times. Each time they listen with the same enjoyment without getting bored. When parents try to shorten the story by leaving out a passage or even just a few words, children immediately notice this and insistently correct their parents. However, when children do **not** enjoy having stories read to them, this may be a sign that they do not have the necessary auditory memory abilities rather than any issues with concentration. Our working memory is the foundation of auditory concentration. Children whose auditory memory does not work well quickly forget what happened in a story just heard. Naturally, they quickly lose any enjoyment in listening, as for them listening to a story does not generate a movie in the mind. Of course, the affected children cannot explain this to the adults in their lives. They simply live with the unexplained fact that stories simply make little sense to them and that it is no fun to listen to someone who is talking a lot.

AUDITORY WORKING MEMORY IS THE FOUNDATION OF AUDITORY CONCENTRATION.

Disorders of Auditory and Speech Processing due to Temporary Hearing Impairment

When children have frequent and recurring middle ear infections in their preschool years, they also endure a period of hearing impairment with each infection. Since there are critical phases of the development of speech and auditory processing, these periods of hearing impairment can lead to problems or delays in speech development and central auditory and speech processing – disorders that often go undetected for a long time.

The typical symptoms of central auditory processing disorder (CAPD), which will be described in more detail later, are significant impairments in the auditory working memory, which naturally leads to serious difficulties in learning to read and write. For example, to write the word **lemon** correctly

SPELL THE WORD LEMON

we must analyze its five phonological elements and write them down in the correct sequence. A six-year-old child whose working memory normally can accommodate six items of information will easily manage this task. However, children with a central auditory processing disorder may be able to accommodate only three items in their working memory. As soon as a fourth one is added, the items already stored fall out of their correct sequence. As a result, the affected children can no longer tell how the sequence of letters started and lose orientation. They often write the letters they have so laboriously analyzed before in the now disordered sequence, in this case **leomn**, capturing some of the sounds they remember but forgetting others entirely.

WHEN CHILDREN WITH CAPD TRY TO READ A LONGER WORD, SUCH AS CROCODILE, THEY CANNOT SUCCEED AT ALL.

Children with the above-described disorder run into problems even though they know the individual letters and can read them in the correct sequence with correct pronunciation. However, as soon as they come upon a word with more than three letters, their working memory fails, and they no longer know what letter they started with when spelling out the word. Not surprisingly, they cannot reassemble the letters to form the word. Instead, they are left with a random jumble of letters that makes no sense to them.

Children struggling with a central auditory processing disorder then often resort to guessing, or they try to give up "that reading thing" and avoid it whenever possible. Understandably, they often have temper tantrums when they are forced to practice reading and feel nearly engulfed by the underlying despair. Children, like their parents and teachers, do not understand why they cannot learn to read well despite their best efforts.

1.08
RECOGNIZING WORDS AT A GLANCE: SIMULTANEOUS VISUAL PERCEPTION

When children have learned the letters of the alphabet and can properly map speech sounds (phonemes) onto letter shapes, they have developed reliable grapheme-phoneme correspondence. Once they can reassemble longer words from the individual letters without any problems, children begin to develop visual abilities that allow them to grasp entire words at a glance. This ability to correctly grasp complex visual information all at once – that is, truly at one glance – is called simultaneous visual perception.

For example, most beginning readers first laboriously spell out the word **crocodile**, and then can relatively quickly and reliably recognize the identical word when they see it again two lines later. This recognition is based on visual details and the contours of the letter combination, which by then looks already familiar to them because it was stored in short-term memory. Seeing the same word again, the brain signals "I have seen this before, the word is crocodile."

As you can see, this ability speeds up the reading process considerably. Indeed, it allows recognition at a speed that is closer to that of normal speech flow than the slow, laborious process of spelling out a word again and again. Clearly, simultaneous visual perception speeds up and simplifies reading and comprehension.

Visual simultaneous perception is a very complex brain function that has several essential prerequisites. In particular, symbol recognition, shape recognition, spatial perception and orientation, and a well-functioning visual working memory are indispensable prerequisite functions. When all components are available – in visual **and** language development – simultaneous processing of words is incredibly fast. We can easily process as many as six letters in 100 milliseconds perfectly. Not only do we recognize each word rapidly and correctly but we also **"scan in" details of its correct spelling** at the same time.

In other words, children and adults with perfect simultaneous visual processing quickly come to enjoy reading and at the same time are equipped to capture and retain the visual details of correct spelling while they are reading, without any additional effort. It's as though people who can read that fast have a large visual "spotlight" that allows them to see and read several words at one time. As a result, they may only need to look at a line twice to read it instead of having to track each word.

However, for children whose ability in simultaneous visual perception and processing is not well-developed or developed at all, as it was the case with Mario, reading becomes a very laborious and stressful process, and certainly not something a child would enjoy or like.

Of course, being able to read is an indispensable precondition for successful learning in school, regardless of subject area. Texts and assignment instructions as well as chemical formulas all must be read to be understood. Students who need a long time for reading or make mistakes inevitably have great difficulties in many subjects.

At no other time in history people were reading as much and in so many different ways as we do today. We read **"digitally"** on computer screens, tablets, smartphones, on displays we wear on our wrist. Of course we also still read in the "old-school, **analog** way" on paper, looking at black print on the white pages of newspapers and books. When reading "real" books, we can feel the pages as we turn them, feel the weight of the book in our hands, and know how many pages we have read and how many are still waiting for us.

In addition to using reading as a tool for quickly taking in information, we can also use it for enjoyment and pleasure. When children or adults talk about their most important and memorable reading experiences, it is obvious that being able to immerse themselves for hours in a different world, to engage their imagination through reading, has given them many meaningful, important, and unique experiences. Experiencing another world in our imagination, adopting a different perspective for some time – perhaps that of Harry Potter or Huckleberry Finn – is an important and meaningful pleasure that should be available to all children.

1.09
CONTROLLING EYE MOVEMENTS WHEN READING: THE OCULOMOTOR SYSTEM

Reading is a process that involves eye movements and requires perfect control of the complex oculomotor system, which perfectly coordinates our

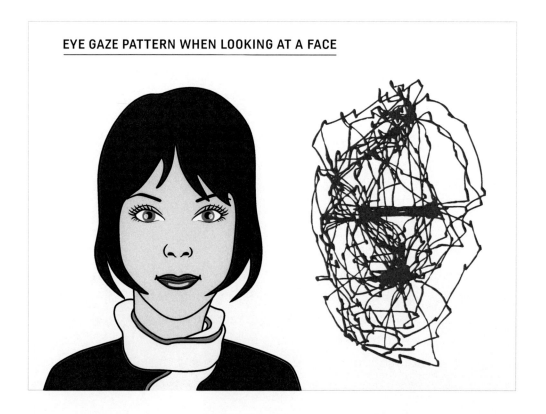

EYE GAZE PATTERN WHEN LOOKING AT A FACE

eyes so they can scan lines of text with absolute precision from left to right. Most of the time we do not even notice that our eyes move at all while we are reading. We simply look at a text and read it – it seems there is not much more to say about it.

However, these abilities are not to be taken for granted. When we get tired quickly from reading, we may not know that our problems are related to the regulation of our eye movements. Because vision and eye movements are so closely interrelated, we tend to experience them as if they were one process. This is accurate perception.

Our eyes are always and constantly in motion. 12 eye muscles ensure that we can look up, down, right, and left with both eyes in a coordinated fashion. Usually, we fix our gaze on a point for only 0.2 seconds before moving on to the next point. Our eyes move very rapidly between fixations or movements we do not notice. These brief "saccades" follow rapidly one upon the other at speeds of up to **0.31 miles or about 1,640 feet per second**. During these movements perception is suppressed. If that were not the case, we would see only a "blurred" image. Our eyes "scan" our environment with these rapid zigzag movements, and the brain subsequently combines the many tiny image segments into one overall impression.

Thus, every time we recognize a shape, a complex process of very rapid, very precise scanning movements of the eyes is involved. Characteristic details bearing important information are scanned very rapidly and repeatedly so that no important changes are overlooked. For example, when we communicate with other people, it is of utmost importance, indeed crucial, that we are able to perceive and interpret their facial expressions correctly.

We can tell almost instantaneously what a person's mood is just from looking at the facial expression and the eyes and mouth. From that brief but important impression we know whether we can engage in a relaxed conversation or whether we need to be cautious. The pattern our gazes follow when looking at faces is almost identical to the one our nearest relatives, the great apes, use when communicating with other members of their tribe. For example, when eye movements of a chimpanzee looking at another chimpanzee are recorded, we find very black areas around the eyes and mouth indicating that the viewer's gaze rested on these spots repeatedly and for a particularly long time. Similarly in humans the constant movement of our eye muscles is the basis of accurate recognition and vision. **Only a moving eye can see shapes!** When eye muscles are temporarily rendered immobile in experiments, vision is no longer possible, and the person cannot see despite a perfectly functioning retina. To see at all, we must be able to move our eyes to scan contours and details. Without that eye movement, we see not even black shadows,but rather nothing at all.

Mario is looking forward to goingtoschool becau se there he willfina lly learn to readand write. Youne ed to know a lot of let ters to readall the won derful books they ha vein the library.

Usually, our eye movements cover a relatively large area. Just think of your field of vision when scanning your surroundings in traffic in order to deter-mine your position on the road, the speed of other road users, and the course of the road so you can identify potential obstacles and hazards quickly and adjust your own or your vehicle's movements. Likewise, children looking at a picture book use similar large-scale gazes or saccades as they scan the pages. Reading, however, presents very different challenges regarding the coordination of our eye muscles. Now our eye movements must coordinate micromovements that adapt to the line of text read. Writing runs horizontally across the page and consists of letters tightly arranged side by side in letter sequences that are scanned and read from left to right. Subjectively, we have the impression that our eyes move smoothly and steadily along the line. However, in reality our eyes execute very rapid "jumps" that are called reading saccades. This movement pattern is not innate but must be learned. Once we have learned to read, our eyes can continuously move this way for many hours without getting the least bit tired.

However, for beginning readers in elementary school who have problems controlling their eyes' horizontal micromovements and reading saccades, learning to read will be very difficult. If the required movement pattern is not yet available, or if it cannot be learned properly because undiagnosed problems with eye muscle coordination prevent perfectly coordinated horizontal scanning movements, the child's eyes and, indeed, entire body will tire very quickly. When these children try to read, their eye movements often do not come to rest at points that match the segmentation of printed words. As a result, these children get confused because the letter combination where their gaze lands does not make sense.

For example, instead of landing on the first letter of a word, the child's gaze may come to rest on the third letter or perhaps on the word after the next. When moving from one line to the next, the child may skip the first word, or the gaze may slide onto a line below the next. Obviously, after a few lines this entire process becomes a tiring effort, and the text no longer makes any sense.

1.10
DEVELOPING AN EFFECTIVE SIGHT WORD VOCABULARY

Have you ever learned a foreign language, and did you take classes in spelling that language? Have you ever taken remedial classes in spelling a foreign language? If not, isn't it surprising that school-age children spend four years in elementary school learning how to spell their first language, usually their native tongue, but in subsequent years the very complicated spelling of a foreign is no longer taught this way?

Rather, students in foreign language classes in high school are simply instructe to study and memorize their vocabulary without being given any explanation of how to learn the correct spelling of foreign words that are often pronounced differently from the way they are spelled – and based on different rules than the ones they know from their own language.

Students can succeed at this only if they have a very precise visual memory for word images and sequences of letters that follow very different pronunciation rules than their own language. Children trying to work by ear, saying foreign words out loud and then writing them phonetically, make many mistakes and have trouble learning a foreign language. Indeed, many children do not even learn correct spelling of their native language in elementary school. As a result, they develop poor spelling habits that take years of special classes at school and therapy in special learning centers to correct.

Can you tell how you manage to check if the sentence you see on the right is spelled correctly? Most likely, you will do what you always do when checking spelling: **you look it up**. And you did this in your brain, which contains a sort of visually scanned dictionary – or perhaps you look up the word in a printed dictionary or on your computer's spell checker.

That is, while you are reading, your visual brain is constantly checking whether the text is spelled correctly. In this process you are using your simultaneous visual perception – reading words, in your native or a foreign language, and recognizing them and remembering how to pronounce them. At the same time, details of the spelling and visual features of the words are stored in your visual memory.

How do yu indetefy
spel in erors ?

Scanning and taking in all relevant spelling information in one step is an extremely complex ability of our visual system, one that is very useful for learning. Thanks to this ability we can develop a visual dictionary in our brain that stores the correct spelling of words as we read them, parallel to the reading process.

This visually stored spelling dictionary in our brain is also very useful in checking texts for errors because it is already automatically working while we are reading the text. Teachers would not be able to correct and grade numerous student papers if for each mistake they first had to think about what spelling rule had been ignored there. This type of analysis would take way too much time and would require that several brain areas devote energy and effort to this task. It is much more practical and efficient to use the visually stored dictionary in our brain. Much like computer spell check programs – only much, much faster – our brain's dictionary function alerts us when we read something that is spelled wrong or has other errors. It takes less than 10 milliseconds to recognize that a word looks wrong.

Visual Spelling Scanner versus Years of Drilling Spelling Rules

As you may know from experience, it takes some time to select the correct spelling of a word among the many suggestions offered by a spell check program if you do not already know the correct spelling. That is precisely the situation children with dyslexia face. After years of drilling, they have memorized every spelling rule and still have countless errors in each writing and dictation exercise. The speed at which teachers dictate and children therefore must write is much too fast for them to think about and apply spelling rules simultaneously. No brain can do that much at once.

Many children with dyslexia can invent and tell wonderful stories. But when they have to write their stories down, they are afraid of having to correct a lot of spelling errors. Even though in terms of language and intellectual skills they are capable of filling endless pages with creative and humorous texts, they prefer to summarize their stories in three short sentences to avoid errors, and thus develop a minimalist writing style.

Being able to see quickly at a glance what words look like and which are misspelled confers an enormous advantage. The visual spelling scanner in our brain indeed makes all the processes involved in learning to spell easier, simplified, and almost effortless.

This is the very same scanner you would use to learn French or any other foreign language. Without this visual scanner it is extremely difficult to learn the spelling of foreign languages for it is not enough to know spelling rules. Instead, we must see the words spelled correctly to store them in our memory. Our visual spelling scanner works with such great precision that we usually are not even aware of it being at work.

Have you ever not been sure about how to spell a word and had no dictionary at hand to help you? Did you then resort to the technique of simply writing the word in the two or three versions you think might be correct and found very quickly, that you simply knew with certainty which version was correct? Perhaps you cannot explain how you knew, but your choice is the correct one. In such situations you are experiencing your visually scanned spelling dictionary at work.

How Would You Learn Correct Spelling without this Visual Ability?

Imagine that reading is very difficult for you, and so you avoid it as much as possible. Without you being aware of it, your word image scanner is not working or is working so slowly that it only takes in **two or three letters in 800 milliseconds**. The other kids in your class have a scanner that takes in **twice as many letters in only 100 milliseconds** – that is, their scanners work eight times faster than yours. The other children thus learn effortlessly how to spell – in passing, so to speak – while they are reading and without particularly noticing it. They have fun doing it and enjoy reading stories in books.

You, however, must practice and practice and practice some more just to learn how to spell simple words. When your very slow spelling scanner happens to scan words imprecisely or wrongly, then stores them incorrectly, this inevitably develops into a form of dyslexia.

YOU
MUST PRACTICE
AND PRACTICE
AND
PRACTICE

2

Chapter

Neuropsychology
of Vision

2

NEUROPSYCHOLOGY
OF VISION

2.01
WHAT IS VISUAL PERCEPTION?

In chapter 1 you have seen how important visual perception is for a child's overall development and ability to learn. But what exactly happens during visual perception? To get an answer we do not have to look at Ophthalmology but rather at Psychology and Neuropsychology in particular.

Neuropsychologists have been studying for decades how the brain processes information in order to understand the individual components of the highly complex process of visual perception. Their insights are useful in diagnosing disorders in the brain's information processing functions, and in developing therapies for them.

This special area of research and therapy is more the domain of clinical vision scientists than in the training of eye doctors. Therefore interdisciplinary dialogue in this regard are still rare, as many eye doctors do not recognize when disorders of visual processing exist, and so cannot help children suffering from these disorders. The exception to this is a specialized group of eyedoctors known as developmental optometrists.

This is How Visual Perception Works

It is easier to understand how visual perception works if you do a little exercise in self-observation. Give yourself some time and allow yourself to fully enjoy the process of image recognition because you will have this experience only

OPTICAL ILLUSION

once in your life. To fully experience the effect, please do not continue to read until after you have tried this exercise, as the proceeding text promises to be a spoiler.

If you observe yourself closely while looking at this picture, you will notice that your eyes move across the surface of the picture, searching. Initially, your eyes will process white and black spots of various sizes placed randomly on the page, with some spots connected to each other. After looking at the image for some time, you will see the spots beginning to form a pattern. Either gradually or all of a sudden, in a flash, you will see that this is a picture of a Dalmatian, and at the same time you will even notice the image's spatial depth.

Interestingly, once our brain has recognized an image, it does not return to the state of nonrecognition. If you look at the same picture again in five minutes, you will see and recognize what is shown here in a matter of milliseconds.

Paintings that do not show clearly recognizable objects are categorized as "abstract art" or "nonrepresentational painting." When this type of painting was first introduced around 1910, it caused protests and scandals. From the psychological perspective this is unsurprising. After all, when we look at something, we want to know **what** we are looking at. We want to be able to see what **it means** – that is what visual perception is all about.

In other words, visual perception is the recognition and understanding of what we see. In fact, we are constantly moving our eyes, sweeping them across shapes, looking for meaning and context. Only when we find these things, we feel that we have really seen something.

Seeing is an active and intelligent process that involves the construction and interpretation of images by our eyes and our brain. The French philosopher Merleau-Ponty most astutely describes the complicated process of seeing when he says: "Vision is the brain's way of touching the world." That is, with every look we are engaging in recognition and understanding. We recognize

objects, people, processes, and sequences of events taking place over time and space, and on that basis we develop experiential models of our world.

Vision is High-Performance Information Processing

Neurobiologists, perceptual psychologists, physicists, and specialists in computer-aided vision have spent decades studying how light stimuli reaching the retina of our eyes can lead to a world of images in our heads. In the past twenty years knowledge about this process has grown immensely. Billions of neurons in our brain are dedicated to the processing of visual information. In this process our eyes have more processing power than the fastest supercomputer, and so it is not surprising that the world-wide research into retina prosthesis has yet to be completed. Ultimately, such a computer chip has to take over the functions of destroyed retina cells in order to enable blind people to see again.

As sighted people, we only need to open our eyes in order to see colorful landscapes with various depths dimensions, to see art works or simply our living room, the computer screen or the book we are reading now. Forms, colors, shading, movements, surface textures, individual objects, or entire visual scenes – all are recognizable for us because they are constructed and interpreted by our brain in accordance with certain principles.

At the level of retinal receptors, however, we have nothing more than a **mosaic of individual states of excitation** that are either switched **on** or **off**. Our visual perception is based on points of light that are constantly active and changing in both space and time. You can picture your retina and the areas of the brain where the primary visual information is processed as an electronic display or score board, much like the ones seen at airports or on billboards.

Countless points of light that are active or passive at various points in time organize and reorganize themselves in patterns in just milliseconds. In other words, the retina is intrinsically a part of the brain located just outside of it. Its task is to capture those streams of light and dark points in its network of receptors. This network of receptors is organized into a coordinate system that allows us to pinpoint the location of objects we see.

Pictures of shapes, figures, contours, lines, or contrasts do not yet appear on the retina itself – even motion is not perceived until a later stage in the process of seeing. Beyond the activity of the retinal receptor cells, seeing requires learning processes. For example, we must learn through experience, which combinations of characteristics regularly occur at the same location at the same time and can be expected.

As we go through life, we get to know the characteristic features of objects, and learn to recognize them. Clearly, remembering earlier impressions is a very important part of our perception in the present. It is the experience of recognition that establishes the reliability, repeatability, and predictability of our perceived reality and thus, also our accompanying sense of order and security. Ultimately it is in seeing the world, that we learn to understand it.

This close connection between seeing and understanding is also reflected in language. For example, we say "I see" to indicate that we have fully understood something or we talk about having "insights" or "perspective." Likewise, the affinity between seeing and thinking is expressed in terms such as "point of view" and "worldview."

2.02
COMPONENTS OF VISUAL PERCEPTION PROCESSING

The enormous significance of visual perception for learning has been descri-bed in chapter 1. Now you will learn more about some basic elements of visual processing, such as spatial perception and orientation, shape recognition, figure-ground perception, visual orientation, and the ability to visualize.

What is recognition of visual-spatial relationships and visual-spatial orientation?

If your child has trouble recognizing the letters of the alphabet, you may have heard about problems in the recognition of visual-spatial relationships and orientation or through a doctor's or occupational therapist's diagnosis about your child. Most of the time, no additional information is provided to explain what exactly the term and the diagnosis mean. For the most part you are told that your child cannot do something as well as other children can.

The ability to recognize visual-spatial relationships and spatial orientation is defined as the ability of our visual information processing system to interpret the **spatial orientation of objects and abstract symbols in relation to an axis**. For example, if you look at a chair standing to your right and then turn quickly around pivoting 180 degrees (a one-half turn), you will see the chair on your left side instead of the right side. This is how our body's position establishes the relative position of objects as being to our right or left hand side.

Of course, it's a very different matter for letters of the alphabet and numbers. Regardless of my angle of vision, the letter **b** has a predefined shape with a "bulge" that must always be to the right of the vertical line. If you see the symbol the other way around, that is, with the bulge to the left of the vertical line, you are looking at a different letter – a **p** is not the same as a **q**. Children can learn their letters and numbers only if they can be sure in their assessment of the spatial position and orientation of symbols consisting of lines and curves that are always arranged in a certain relationship to each other. As long as children are not sure in this and confuse these characteristics of symbols, learning to read and write will be a great struggle for them.

To recognize the spatial orientation of symbols we need to have a general visual spatial orientation. While this is a basic function of seeing, it is a very complex phase in the development of perception, one that may be difficult even for adults. For example, just think of the last time you tried to give directions to a particular place or tried to follow someone else's confusing directions. If we want to give someone detailed directions on how to get from point A to point B, we must be able to visualize both places on a virtual inner map before our mind's eye. Moreover, we must be able to put ourselves in the position of the other person, who is to move on the basis of that virtual map that exists only within our imagination. We must provide that person with information that makes correct navigation to the destination possible. We do this by using the correct linguistic codes so that the other person can develop in his or her mind's eye a memory and image of a sequence of events and movements: "Turn left onto the second cross street, and then go straight to the next traffic light; turn right and then immediately turn left again. The entrance is on the left side of the red house behind the gas station."

NUMBER COLUMNS – SPATIAL ORIENTATION

Clearly, it's easy to understand why we may prefer to delegate these complex tasks of visual orientation to our modern navigation systems. The success of these devices is surely in part due to the fact that many adults have limited or insufficient abilities when visual-spatial orientation is concerned. In particular the matching of a two-dimensional map of a region and their own real position in an unfamiliar three-dimensional world proves most difficult. We find it easier to rely on electronic devices for navigating to our destinations. These devices are easy to use and require no imagination or visualization efforts on our part; they simply tell us when to turn where.

At this point, it is compelling to reflect on how we have developed the ability to use the concepts **left** and **right**, as this opens up a vast field of complicated visual processing considerations. As you may know from your own experience or from other people, not all adults have a firm grasp of these concepts.

Helping children overcome weaknesses in visual-spatial orientation and helping them use the corresponding concepts correctly can also be part of the Optometric Vision Therapy that will be described in more detail later. The training that is part of this therapy can help children become visibly more self-confident; after all, being able to orient ourselves properly in space, grounds us and gives us security.

What is involved in figure-ground perception?

Perhaps you have heard one of your loved ones say: "Nothing to eat here – again!" as they look into the fridge, ignoring their favourite yoghurt because a jar of pickles was partially hiding it. Or perhaps you have been looking for your spouse in a crowd at the mall, or you could not find your glasses even though they were lying directly in front of you, on a desk overflowing with papers and files. Or you have had the relatively common experience of having forgotten where exactly in a big parking lot you left your car, and now you have find it among very many others that mostly look alike. At least for this situation we now have technological aids; we can send a radio signal to our car via the remote control and breathe a sigh of relief when the car answers with a chirpy beep and eagerly flashing lights to show us the way.

The ability to **recognize something familiar among competing shapes, colors, and figures** is called figure-ground perception, and to develop it we must be able to recognize objects as shapes that stand out among the mass of other shapes surrounding them. Since we do not live in white empty space but in a world filled with countless objects, this is an extremely important visual ability. The phrase "they cannot see the forest for the trees" is used to describe people who have trouble with figure-ground perception, and figuratively applies also when a multitude of sensory impressions causes us to lose sight of what is important to us.

Children whose figure-ground perception is poorly developed find it difficult to deal with "crowded" worksheets, especially when pictures and several smaller text passages are scattered across the sheet and obscure the crucial assignments and instructions. It is all too easy then, for these kids to overlook assignments or test questions as they take more time to find the information they need.

It may take some persuasion to get teachers to change the design of their work materials, but when teachers agree to provide changes and accommo-

**CANNOT SEE THE FOREST
FOR THE TREES.**

dations for children struggling with visual limitations, the results are often surprising. In Math, for example, instead of the typical worksheet design with eight or more tasks per page, teachers should redesign the sheets with only two tasks per page and use large fonts for children with weak figure-ground perception. With simple adjustments such as these, children can improve their performance by as much as two letter grades.

Even the design of the children's notebooks can play an important role. Children who have difficulties with figure-ground perception can get confused by lined notebook pages that include three additional aid lines. Intended to help children to correctly place the descenders and ascenders of various letters, these extra lines add to the busy background and make it harder for children with weak figure-ground perception to see the letters correctly. As a result, learning to write becomes difficult for them. Parents and teachers are often surprised to find that a simple change such as using notebooks with simple lines on a white page can avoid visual confusion and help the affected children improve their writing.

2.03
WHAT IS VISUALIZATION?

To learn successfully children must develop the ability to remember what they have seen and then be able to call that to mind as an inner picture at any time – that is, they must be able to visualize. The ability to visualize can become an extraordinarily important tool for learning. For example, it allows us to remember a mental image of a word and effectively recall the correct spelling of a word once we have seen it. This is indispensable when learning to spell as well as in learning a foreign language in which words are spelled very differently from the way they sound and pronunciation rules are also different from those of the student's own language. In Geography lessons visualization helps children to develop an image of the world; visualization enables children to understand the setup of experiments, chemical formulas and the periodic table, and to work with mathematical formulas or learn geometry.

Of course, visualization is also an important tool in many other situations. Visualization has become a popular tool among the world's top athletes. For example, before a decisive race, a world-class racecar driver will visualize the race track, the actions to be taken, and the win. Just before the start of many sporting events and competitions, athletes, with their eyes closed, may move around in odd ways. They are visualizing the course of the competition or match, the routes, reactions, perhaps the perfect throw. Perhaps they already see themselves in their mind's eye standing on the winners' podium and accepting a medal. What these athletes are doing is much like attentively **watching an imaginary movie in their head, a movie they have created themselves.**

Visualization is a state of consciousness people have used for centuries in meditation and rituals. Nowadays we use this ability in psychotherapy and coaching. As we close our eyes and imagine a picture, a sequence of movements or actions we will take, this inner picture or movie influences our brain. We can improve movement sequences with the help of our imagination, and with frequent repetition we can even make these movements automatic.

The creation of inner images involves and activates the same areas of the brain that would be used for the activity itself. Through repetition – whether in reality or in the imagination – the neural pathways necessary for these movements are stimulated and stabilized so that we can get better at the skills we are practicing. For example, researchers have found that just imagining we are playing a piece of music on the piano physically changes our brain in the areas controlling complex coordinated movements of our fingers.

In another example, consider chess players; those who excel in strategy use their visualization skills to think several moves ahead and anticipate the opponent's counter attacks. They apply the demanding and sophisticated cognitive function of taking the perspective of another as own. Players not only anticipate their own perspective and sequence of moves on the chess board; they must also be able to imagine which moves their opponents might choose based on the opponents' perspective. Of course, chess players have to keep all this in mind without losing track of their own potential moves. Clearly, chess players need not only good **spatial imagination** involving various perspectives but also an excellent **visual sequential memory for movements and positions.**

Another important visual capacity is the ability to imagine a two-dimensional or three-dimensional object and to rotate that object mentally, therefore to be able to "see" it from several different angles in a process called **mental rotation**. Psychologists consider this ability an **essential factor of intelligence** and have therefore included such tasks in many intelligence tests.

Can preschoolers visualize? Yes, of course! Just watch kindergartners when they are engaged in role play, and you will see extensive imagination and visualization at work as children assign each other – and objects – various roles:

"NOW YOU BE THE ROBBER."

"LET'S PLAY — THIS STONE HERE CAN BE OUR BABY."

"AND NOW LET'S PLAY, THE STONE IS A BOAT."

Children think up and act out countless variations of situations and stories. Their games include trying out different roles or identities for persons, objects, or places, identities they easily change at will. Even when children merely listen to a story being told or read, visualization is involved. The more intense and detailed the virtual movie in their mind, the greater the enjoyment.

Do We Need Visualization for Learning?

Yes, of course! Textbooks and teachers all use concrete visual means to illustrate or explain something. They use mind maps, symbols, illustrations, diagrams, lists, family trees, clusters, or central figures with connecting lines and expect students to understand the information and remember it.

2.04
HOW VISUAL PERCEPTION DEVELOPS

As part of our overall development, visual perception develops together with our motor skills in infancy and early childhood. You will learn about this in more detail in the following section, and in the process you will also understand why Vision Therapy calls for movement of the whole body and involves movement exercises.

Imagine a tripod with a precision camera mounted on it. The tripod represents your body, and the precision camera stands in for the functions of your eyes. If the tripod wobbles, even with the best precision camera, the picture quality will be poor. The same is true for your child's body. To make perfect vision possible, our body must be motionless in some situations, must have a stable equilibrium, and must have well controlled motor functions.

If your child shows any unusual motor behavior and is prescribed seemingly strange balance and movement exercises in therapy, read on and you will learn the reasons behind those exercises. If your child is not affected, you can skip this chapter.

Early Phase of Visual Information Processing

In the earliest phases of our development as infants, we are focused on touching, moving, and getting to know our own body. After some time, we begin to experience our body's **bilateral organization**, an experience that is essential for visual development.

Our body is bilaterally symmetrical, and we can picture it split in half down the middle by a vertical axis. On each side of our body we have two movement elements (arms and legs) and paired organs of perception (eyes, nostrils, and ears).

The organs responsible for our breathing, fluid balance, and reproductive system are also paired and in a sense provide their own backup. Even our brain is a divided organ, not just virtually but in reality: a deep sulcus separates the hemispheres of the brain.

Anatomically, the paired functions of perception – movement (including our motor activities), seeing, hearing, smelling, and touching – are also doubled functions of our nervous system, with many crossings and recrossings of neural pathways interconnecting all processes.

A BRAIN OF TWO HALVES

How do we become aware of the two halves of our body in infancy?

While we are still in our mother's womb, our uncoordinated arm and leg movements, such as kicking, boxing, or pushing ourselves off from something, give us an early experience of the ways we can move our body. Early experiences with the sense of touch allow us to feel ourselves in relation to the world "out there," a world that is still very confined at that stage.

After birth, many newborns can search with their eyes for their mother's face as early as on the first day of life and even fix their eyes briefly on her. After that, the infant's little eyes roll on, seemingly in an uncoordinated fashion, and a reason why some infants look cross-eyed.

As infants, with our every look that reaches its goal and briefly "holds" it, we develop complex neural pathways that promote development of coordinated movement of the external eye muscles and happens as a result of seeing and recognizing objects. To fuse the functions of the two eyes located a small distance apart from each other into one sensorimotor unit of both perception and movement, requires interconnecting an enormous number of neurons, all working at the same time. We learn, practice, and master this task in infancy with our every look.

During that phase, when our hands happen to touch an object, our grasp reflex ensures that we hold on to it. In a later phase of infancy, we move the object to our mouth to explore it further because the mouth is our most essential area of perception at that age.

With every eye contact, every loving hold and touch we experience at that early age that our attachment to those taking care of us deepens. Long before we can move our body at will, we develop the ability to follow our familiar caregivers with our eyes. Not long after that, we become able to seek out objects we are interested in by looking with both eyes together. We **fixate** on objects with our gaze and can even grasp them with both hands. Eyes and hands work simultaneously together from left to right to locate objects and draw them towards the middle or center of our body.

The sensorimotor process of **simultaneously perceiving and moving**, such as grasping with both hands or looking with both eyes at the same object, enables us to initiate deliberate action. From here we can explore objects through a process of perceiving, grasping and looking. When we are awake during this phase of infancy, we are always busy with drawing objects closer to ourselves, pulling them actively into our own radius of perception and movement. Through countless repetitions of this process we get to know the objects around us.

In addition, we are engaged in a constant process of discovering ways of moving our body. Raising and turning our head, grasping and pulling things toward ourselves, pushing ourselves off with our feet, crawling. These movements are initiated and accompanied by visual impressions and the development of coordinated eye movements. Looking at the same object with both eyes at the same time, and following the object's movement with our eyes, all these are highly complex brain functions that give our attention direction and goals long before we can move our body deliberately and freely by crawling.

Our innate grasp reflex initially allows us to hold on to objects. Later we develop the ability to explore objects deliberately and accidentally letting go of an object, losing it, and then finding it again. If you watch this process, you will see how much infants enjoy this game of holding on, letting go, and finding again. For caregivers, this marks the beginning of a somewhat strenuous time, for the letting go soon turns into actively letting drop and then into throwing. As a result of countless repetitions of this process, we learn to experience space, and our radius of perception and action steadily expands.

Our Experience of Space Varies Widely

We distinguish between different dimensions of space. For example, we each have our own personal space, the space immediately around us. We keep most people at a greater distance and feel uncomfortable if they come too close. You know how uncomfortable you feel when uninvited strangers invade your personal space like in a crowded elevator. In such situations people have to stand much closer to each other than most are comfortable with. Many find it helpful then to avoid eye contact and thus maintain at least some sort of distance.

How much personal space people need to feel comfortable varies and may depend on their cultural context. For example, the boundary of our personal space, the line we do not want strangers to cross, is much closer to our body if we live in densely populated areas than if we inhabit more spacious and less populated regions of the world.

The nontactile, **extrapersonal space** can only be grasped visually and is clearly outside our physical reach.

The term **peripersonal space** designates the area that is defined by the reach of our hands, that is, an arm's length. This is the area we explore intensely in childhood. Our first experiences of space, of near and far, next to, above or under enables us to integrate our own position into the space around us, even before we can move independently through that space. As soon as we have learned to turn around on our own and can lift ourselves up, we advance into our environment by creeping, crawling, and finally walking. This marks the beginning of a more intense phase of learning about space and the objects in our world. With great enthusiasm we grasp everything within our reach and continue exploring with our eyes, hands, and mouth. Even many years later, some children still need to use their hands when trying to grasp new infor-mation. They simply have to touch everything. They often ignore their parents' reminder to "only look at it with your eyes!" because the exploratory behavior of early childhood is such a powerful driving force.

As children mature, this developmental phase of having to touch everything will be replaced gradually with a phase where children can gaze and classify objects without needing to touch them. For example, at the age of one, children can already move around and navigate quite purposefully in a three-dimensional visual world; they can look at objects, recognize them, and grasp them.

At the age of four months, infants already use their brains to construct object boundaries and can distinguish different objects from each other. At four or five months old, infants can grasp in a rudimentary way basic physical principles based on perspective, shading, partial covering up of surfaces, etc. For example, one such principle is that two objects cannot simultaneously occupy the same space.

Many processes of visual information processing are established and learned during this developmental phase

In particular, shape and object recognition and figure-ground perception are abilities that enable us to identify individual objects in the presence of countless other shapes and colors, and to focus our attention on the items we choose.

Spatial orientation is the ability to integrate our own body into the space around us. For example, when we want to grasp an object located on our right, we turn our body in that direction. We stretch our arms above our head to grasp an object within our reach. We turn around when something interesting is happening behind us. We can assess about how far away from us distant objects are and whether we have to move in that direction to be able to reach them.

For example, as we learn that our mother is still our mother even when we see her only from the side or from behind, or that the ball we have touched before is still as soft and smooth when we touch it again, we develop a bond of trust in the people and the world around us. In this process, a foundation is laid for basic trust, for security and confident familiarity with our surroundings. The more we become familiar with the world around us, the faster we can recognize, classify and add to our experiences.

Disorders of Perceptual Development

In some forms of autism, infants affected become upset and respond with panic during the very early phases of perceptual development. They do not develop stable figure-ground perception, spatial orientation, and object constancy, and as a result even the smallest changes in visual perspective can be very confusing and upsetting. Lacking repeated experiences of object recognition, they struggle to develop basic trust and secure bonding.

In fact, there is even a visual processing disorder that affects only the identification and recognition of human faces. This "face blindness" or **prosopagnosia** is a congenital disorder and leads to an inability to recognize human faces. Scientists studying this disorder estimate that about 2 percent of all people are affected by it.

However, the name of the disorder, "face blindness" is somewhat misleading. People with this disorder can indeed see faces and can distinguish between faces of men and those of women. They can identify the emotional expression on these faces as well as other visual and emotional facial features. However, what they cannot do is recognize other people by their face alone.

The cause for this disorder lies in a tiny region of the brain called the **fusiform gyrus**, also known as the occipitotemporal gyrus. It's specialized cells are dedicated exclusively to the recognition of human facial features. Clearly, this small area of the brain is of utmost importance for our emotional security in communicating with our fellow human beings. Just imagine you had to rely only on voice, movement style, or on entirely external features, such as clothing or hairdo, to be able to tell whether the person you're talking to is your child or your spouse. In that case you would also not be able to recognize your child in a group of children if your child has accidentally put on another child's jacket in kindergarten and is not moving or talking at the moment.

It is important to keep in mind that prosopagnosia is not an emotional disorder; it is also not the same as the problem we all encounter when see someone we know but whose name we cannot remember at the moment. Rather, prosopagnosia is an isolated disorder of visual perception that is not yet fully understood. Many of the people affected by this disorder do not even know that it exists and that they are suffering from it; they just feel uncomfortable and insecure around others without knowing what causes those feelings. Others experience people affected by face blindness as strange, impolite, unfriendly, or uncommunicative because they fail to greet acquaintances.

It is possible that children who act "strangely" when communicating with people outside the comfortable circle of family and friends, or experience anxiety in crowded settings, clinging in panic to their mother's hand to make sure not to lose her, suffer from such a disorder. Moreover, it is important for

AS MANY AS 2 PERCENT OF ALL PEOPLE ARE AFFECTED BY PROSOPAGNOSIA AND WOULD NOT BE ABLE TO RECOGNIZE THEIR OWN CHILD IN A GROUP OF CHILDREN BASED ON THE CHILD'S FACE.

teachers to be informed about these disorders. If the estimate of as many as 2 percent of afflicted persons in the world population is correct, then we can expect that in nearly every school there would be some children suffering from face blindness.

2.05
EARLY SIGNS OF VISUAL INTELLIGENCE AND LOGIC

In recent years scientists have found that the first signs of visual-logical thinking appear very early in infancy. For example, the ability to **recognize the number** of objects reliably and the preconditions for **addition and subtraction** are visual functions and seem to be innate.

To study perceptual processes in infants, scientists make use of the babies' innate visual attention and their willingness to always look eagerly for new impressions and perceptions. Even at the age of only a few weeks, infants can already quickly differentiate between what is familiar to them and what is new. In particular, infants fix their gaze only briefly on what they already know but rest their gaze much longer on new, unfamiliar objects. This ability is called **preferential looking** and offers a way to test infants' visual acuity.

To assess the so-called **number sense** of infants in experiments, researchers show the babies either pictures or objects. For example, infants get to look at images of **two** objects until they are clearly bored. When a new object is added, that is, when there are suddenly **three** objects to look at, the baby is surprised and immediately becomes fully attentive. Infants fix their gaze on familiar objects for about 1.5 seconds, but when they see something new, babies fixate for 3 seconds – twice as long!

Infants, indeed can grasp how many objects there are – the difference between two and three – with one look, and they can express their interest in this through their astonished, intensive gazing. In fact, infants are not interested in things being of different sizes and shapes, but they react very clearly to changes in the number of things they see. Here the rule of "1, 2, 3, many" seems to apply; that is, at that very early age babies "count" no higher than 3.

At the age of four or five months, infants clearly can recognize when basic laws of physics are being violated. For example, when an object that had been lying on a table suddenly floats in the air after the table has been pulled out from under it, even very young babies react with incredulous astonishment and gaze intensely at the object. They respond in the same way when an object that had been concealed behind a screen is not there after the screen has been removed.

Researchers even tried to test whether infants can already grasp the calculation of $1 + 1 = 2$, as described by Stanislas Dehaene in his book "The Number Sense." In that experiment researchers showed five-months-old infants in the lab a small stage with a screen that could be folded up or down. The woman conducting the experiment placed a Mickey Mouse figure on the stage and folded up the screen so that the figure was concealed. Then a hand appeared with a second Mickey Mouse figure, which was also placed behind the screen, and the hand moved away empty. These events are a concrete representation of the addition $1 + 1$. Initially, only one toy was hidden behind the screen, and then a second one was added. The children never saw both Mickey Mouse figures at the same time, but only one after the other.

Would they nevertheless conclude that there should be two Mickey Mouse figures behind the screen?

To find out, the screen was folded away and an unexpected scene was revealed: only one Mickey Mouse figure was there! The children fixed their gaze on this impossible constellation of 1+1=1 for a much longer time than when they were shown the expected result of 1+1=2. In other words, the infants looked at the wrong addition for about 2 seconds longer than at the correct result of 1+1=2.

Likewise, experiments have shown that when infants are paying attention to the number of objects presented, it does not matter to them whether they see the exact same objects. They show no surprise when the objects look different. For example, when in an experiment two teddy bears were concealed behind a screen and then two blue balls were revealed after removal of the screen, the infants did not respond with surprise. In contrast, the babies were clearly surprised when they saw a second teddy bear being placed behind the screen but then saw only one blue ball when the screen was removed. The innate sense demonstrated here for the number of objects (see Dehaene) cannot be deceived by movement nor by changing the identity of the objects shown.

Arithmetic is essentially based on fundamental laws of nature, laws even infants can grasp. For example, an object cannot be in more than one place at the same time, and two objects cannot occupy the same space at the same time. Likewise, an object cannot suddenly disappear and simply reappear again at a different place. Such relocation requires an uninterrupted path of movement through time and space.

These visual abilities present in earliest infancy. Combined with the infant brain's nearly insatiable desire for new perceptions they form an excellent foundation for further development. Seeing is a learning process that begins on the first day of life and is deepened with every new perception!

THE PERFECT FOUNDATION FOR DEVELOPMENT: VISUAL ABILITIES AND A BRAIN WITH AN INSATIABLE DESIRE FOR NEW EXPERIENCES.

2.06
PROGRAMMED FOR DEVELOPMENT:
PRIMARY REFLEXES

The motor development of infants and toddlers is based on innate, involuntary movement programs that run their course automatically. They are set in motion through sensory inputs or changes in the positioning of the body. These reflexes ensure the infant's survival and form the basis for meaningful coordination of limbs, body and head movements. Thus they prove to be fundamental in the development of seeing.

While still in their mother's womb, infants already sense their own movements; they experience gravity by orienting themselves in a very small three-dimensional space and actively perceive equilibrium in a zero-gravity environment. Infants' abilities to hear, touch, and grasp the world have already been prepared before birth. Countless experiences of movement and perception are gathered and processed during the few hours the fetus is awake.

2.07
REFLEXES FOR SURVIVAL

The oral reflexes of searching, sucking and swallowing are present very early on and are trained intensively when the fetus drinks amniotic fluid. Later, in response to tactile stimuli on the cheeks or corners of the mouth, infants turn their head in the direction of the stimulus and open their mouth – a reflex response that is essential for infants' survival and is fully established in the first few hours after birth.

Interestingly, the mouth reflexes are closely connected to movements of hands and feet, and extend to movements of the entire body. A sucking, drinking newborn is working with its entire body and develops a certain tension throughout the entire body, which includes muscle functions. Intensive sucking takes a lot of effort and strength for the newborn. After such a full-body workout, the newborn falls asleep, satisfied, well-trained, and pleasantly tired.

Children who cannot be breastfed and are fed with bottles that have a larger than natural opening compared to the nipple may be prone to muscle weakness. While these bottles may require less sucking effort from the baby, they do not support the child's later development of healthy and vigorous muscle tone.

Our mouth and lip area takes up as much processing space in the brain, specifically in the sensory cortex, as our entire upper body. In addition to being essential for feeding, lips and mouth are also important for exploring objects and later on for our communication through language. Thus, it is unsurprising that they are given that much space and processing power in our brain.

Thanks to the reflexes of hands and feet, infants can clasp and then hold and grasp things. For example, when you gently touch an infant's palm, the baby's

IN THE SENSORY CORTEX MOUTH AND LIPS TAKE UP AS MUCH "PROCESSING SPACE" AS OUR ENTIRE UPPER BODY.

fingers curl into a fist with the thumb bent inward toward the palm. The power involved in this reflex is so great that newborns can be lifted up by their clasped hands. Analogously, when you gently touch the soles of an infant's feet, the baby curls its toes. The clasping reflex of the hands usually disappears about 36 weeks after birth.

During the time when hand and foot reflexes are active intensively, hands, feet, and mouth are closely connected. For example, infants reflexively close their hands into fists when they are sucking and then make kneading motions with their hands in rhythm with the sucking motions of the mouth.

In fact, some reflexes involving the entire body already appear when the fetus is still in the womb. These movement automatisms provide babies with the first experiences of their own body and their own movement; they also support the babies active participation in the birth process.

For example, the **Moro reflex** of newborns is a response to fright and enables the baby to draw its first breath after birth. The reflex can also be observed in our close relatives, the great apes, and ensures their survival by helping to prevent imminent falls: the baby clings reflexively to the mother's fur and utters a cry for help. In humans and great apes, this reflex is essentially a sequence of movements that run their course at great speed. When the reflex causes the nearly spasmodic extension of the limbs and the throwing back of the head, it prepares the infant for breathing and inhaling before crying for help. Subsequently, infants bend their arms and legs into a kind of clutching or holding position, and as they exhale, they cry.

The Moro reflex is triggered by potential dangers in the child's environment, such as sudden noises, sudden bright light, unexpected touch, or changes in position of the head or body. Connected to all sensory channels, this reflex is also accompanied by the release of the stress hormones adrenaline and cortisol that activate the body's generalized autonomic stress response- flight or fight response pattern.

2.08
REFLEXES FOR MOTOR SKILLS DEVELOPMENT

Even while still in their mother's womb, babies show their **asymmetrical tonic neck reflex (ATNR)**, which enables the fetus to extend the arm to the same side in which the head is turned while the arm on the other side flexes toward the back of the head (fencing reflex, fencing position).

This reflex allows infants in the first half year of life to coordinate turning their head, bringing the eyes into the appropriate position to see and prepares the body for grasping with their hands. Thanks to this reflex, infants begin to experience and increasingly become aware of their body's centerline and their movements from right to left. The ATNR also prepares the newborn for the alternating crawling movements of a later developmental phase.

The coordination of head movements, balance, and control of the limbs are reliant on the **tonic labyrinthine reflex (TLR)**, established before birth. Thanks to this reflex, when an infant's head is bent back too far, the baby's arms and legs extend; when the head is bent forward, the babies also bend their arms and legs. In this way the transition is made from the huddled "fetal" position of the unborn child to the stretching out of the body. This transition is initiated purely by movements of the head.

Through the **symmetrical tonic neck reflex (STNR)**, that appears only at a later stage of development, a movement pattern is established allowing infants to move the upper half of their body in relation to the lower half. This reflex is also triggered by moving the head backward or forward. When the head is bent forward and lowered, the child's legs flex. When the head and upper body are upright or slightly bent back, both legs extend.

This reflex program is active only for a short time during infancy and allows infants to get up and move off the floor. Later by rocking forwards and backwards on their hands and knees the STNR is integrated into the totality of the child's movements so that intentional, deliberate and controlled movements of pushing off from a surface are possible. Initially, these attempts cause the infants to slide backward, but eventually they will beginn to crawl forward as well.

When children first stand up from the crawling position and begin to walk freely, we can observe balance responses that look like reflexes; these can still appear later in life in dangerous situations. For example, the **hand-foot-vestibular reflex (HFVR)** ensures that toddlers extend their arms upward or to the side in order to maintain balance when their equilibrium is unstable. These arm movements support the body in maintaining its upright position of standing and its balance when walking.

Children who have not overcome these early balance responses move their arms every time their feet are turned outward or inward. If the feet are rotated inward, then their lower arms and hands rotate outward, and outward rotation of the feet (Charlie Chaplin walk) leads to an inward rotation of arms and hands.

We develop stable and secure equilibrium in our bodily movements when our head movements no longer cause reflexive changes in our muscle tone. The above described reflex patterns provide the raw material for developing movement patterns and motor skills allowing us to move our body, maintain stable balance, and move our head and eyes in a coordinated fashion in all directions. As the reflexes begin to coordinate with our visual perception and our eye-hand position, we gradually develop the ability to grasp and coordinate our limbs for crawling and then walking.

As discussed, our ability to move freely in three-dimensional space develops on the basis of infant reflexes, all of which are triggered and controlled by the position of the head. In particular, the **TLR** enables us to experience the space in front of and behind the body, the **STNR** lets us experience the dimensions of above and below and the **ATNR** allows us to experience the lateral dimensions of right and left. As a result of experiencing these spatial dimensions on our own body, we can then develop the ability to explore and take hold of the three-dimensional space around us. When moving our head no longer triggers large movements of the limbs and we gain full control of our head and body movements along with our posture, then three-dimensional visual perceptual space opens up and gives us overview, orientation, perception of distance and depth, and the freedom of controlled, deliberate action.

In later developmental phases, we **internalize this experience of space into a purely visual imagination** and so create virtual visual objects and set them in motion in our imagination. Likewise, we can visualize the world of numbers and also mentally see rotations of visualized objects. This ability is so fundamentally important for us that we consider it a measure of human intelligence. As mentioned earlier, most intelligence tests employ these crucial tasks of visual-spatial imagination.

2.09
PERSISTENT PRIMARY REFLEXES

Usually, infant reflexes are integrated into the developing flow of deliberate movements, and this integration happens in the first years of life. Reflexes are transformed into increasingly conscious and competent control of our own body and disappear after they have fulfilled their task of preparing us for deliberate and controlled movement.

However, motor development does not run so smoothly for all children. Some children do not fully overcome their reflexes and experience residual reflexes that can persist even beyond the age of ten. If that is the case, these reflexes cause involuntarily triggered muscle tensions that interfere with the children's normal movements. As a result, they have difficulty maintaining balance, are clumsy in their gross and fine motor skills, and cannot fully control the movements of their head, hands, and eyes.

By definition, reflexes are compulsive movements that run their course automatically and outside our awareness. For example, we all know that when doctors tap a spot below the kneecap with their little rubber hammer, they trigger a small reflexive kick. For the most part, we cannot suppress this movement response unless we focus our attention on it. Now just imagine a driver who still has an active persistent impulse of the ATNR so that every time this driver turns his or her head to the left, there is a small impulse to move the right arm that slightly bends that arm and thus threatens to turn the steering wheel to the right. In most cases, people affected by such residual reflexes have no idea why driving is such a strain for them, but it takes a lot of strength and energy to suppress these tiny, entirely unconscious but very disruptive muscle impulses.

When school children have persistent primary reflexes and sudden involuntary muscle movements, they must suppress them, or, even worse, they increase muscle tension throughout their body to prevent involuntary impulses from interfering with their work and classroom activities. Such involuntary movements interfere with planned sequences of actions, such as writing or drawing, and they can cause "clumsiness," such as bumping into things, awkwardness in pouring liquids, and spilling food when eating. **Persistent primary reflexes** are **energy hogs**; counteracting these involuntary motor impulses takes at least as much energy as the planned movement they are disrupting.

Just imagine you are a child with a residual STNR. Every time you bend your head forward to write, you would at the same time have to fight against the extension impulse in your arms. When you copy things from the blackboard , you must look up at the board and down at your notebook repeatedly, each time you would feel this same struggle and eventually find that the muscles in your arms and hands have become sore and irritated. Surely you can understand then that typical disorders of graphomotor coordination – that is, difficulties in using a pencil or pen for writing and drawing – can result in messy, scrawly handwriting that slows down a child's pace of work considerably.

Moreover, since these residual reflexes involve bodily processes from a very early phase in life, processes that are established in our organism long before we are able to speak, it is difficult for the affected children to verbalize their troubles or to understand what is happening to them. Children suffering from persistent primary reflexes struggle to explain to themselves what causes the troubles, and thus they simply become uneasy and insecure regarding certain activities and tasks and try to avoid or resist them. When adults are

SHAPE REPRODUCTION TEST

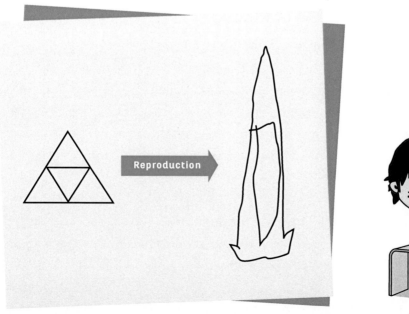

Reproduction

insecure about certain activities, they have an easier time avoiding them entirely than children do when they are still in school. After all, children must write down everything they learn in school, and most teachers require clear legible handwriting. Moreover, children are evaluated in terms of how their work pace compares to the average speed at which their classmates learn and work. Children who consistently work at too slow a pace and with too many errors will face some type of penalty and suffer from stress even more.

In particular, a persisting Moro reflex, which is a fear and startle response that can be triggered by any and all sensory stimuli, can lead to hypersensitivity. Children affected by this quickly feel overwhelmed by sensory impressions; they experience the world as too loud, too bright and too fast. Often they are in a constant state of high alert and have trouble relaxing. Their autonomous nervous system is stuck in a state of constant activation. These children are always nervous, tend to get anxious easily, and find changes in their environment or in established routines very irritating and try to avoid them as much as possible.

Therapists with special training in the field of persistent primary reflexes can diagnose and treat persistent reflexes. Your pediatrician will be a great source for finding such a specialist in your area.

In general, a combination of persistent primary reflexes and disorders of visual perception and binocular functions will have grave and serious effects on school children. Fortunately, there are therapies that have been very successful in helping children overcome these residual reflexes. These therapies are used in our practice in combination with Optometric Vision Therapy. Sequence, method, and combination of therapies must be decided on a case-by-case basis.

2.10
CAN YOUR PRESCHOOLER DO THIS?

Though visual development does not progress at the same pace in all children, preschoolers should have developed the abilities listed below to the point of being able to easily play, do crafts, paint, and move with increasing skill and agility. Children then can easily and securely orient themselves in the various spaces around them, remembering the way to their destination and avoiding obstacles, for example.

The skills preschoolers should have mastered include running, even on sloped paths, running up and down stairs without dragging a foot, swinging on a swing set, hopping on one leg, climbing, balancing, and catching balls. All these tasks require motor coordination and can be mastered successfully thanks to children's sense of balance which should be well-developed by the end of their preschool years alongside their corresponding visual abilities. Mastering tasks requiring fine and complex motor skills, such as buttoning up a shirt, tying shoelaces, pouring a liquid into a glass, or using eating utensils also develops during this time.

Soon children are able to use not only big interlocking Duplo building blocks or bricks but can begin to build free-standing constructions that call for planning, balance, and coordination of various features of different materials. Developing the fine motor skills for hand movements requires good **eye-hand**

COMPLETING A JIGSAW PUZZLE BY LOOKING AT THE PIECES, ANALYZING THEM, AND INSERTING THEM INTO THE CORRECT PLACE IS A VERY DEMANDING VISUAL TASK.

coordination. These skills move from the simple grasping and releasing typical of infancy to preschoolers' ability to hold a wax crayon or even a thin colored pencil to create extensive drawings covering large sheets of paper. Finally, children progress to the level where they can draw fine, thin, and exact lines that prepare them for learning to draw and write later.

By preschool age, children are able to pick up small beads between their thumb and index finger by holding their fingers like tweezers. Preschoolers can then thread the beads on a string and later even create patterns. Likewise, preschoolers can master board games that involve rules for how pieces can move on the board. They can successfully play complicated games such as Memory. Completing a jigsaw puzzle by looking at the pieces, analyzing them, and inserting them into the correct place is a very demanding visual task that involves visual analysis of shapes and well-planned application of motor skills. This strategy is much more complicated than simply moving pieces around and pressing them into spaces where they happen to fit.

In addition, **preschoolers' drawings** also indicate that in their intellectual development they have achieved the capacity for visual abstraction. Children's early doodles and scrawls are "abstract art," but every line already has a meaning and represents themes from the child's experience of the world. For example, a line or a dot can represent an apple, an animal, or even a car. Later, children try their first concrete pictures, often as representations of themselves or their caregivers. They appear as cephalopods, so-called stick figures that consist of a circle and two lines representing the legs. After succeeding with those first recognizable human figures, children place them on all their drawings, repeating them again and again, unless adults encourage them to draw houses or cars.

Graphic representations always have a meaning, and children want to explain them, even when the drawing is nothing more than a few lines or splotches of color. After all, children do not paint for themselves but to communicate, to share themselves. They want more than just praise when they show their pictures to adults. The process of painting or drawing is only complete when the child has communicated something significant to the viewer and when the viewer has understood the child and the meaning of the picture.

The early drawings of young children are reminiscent of the early graphic representations in human history, as found in cave paintings. These paintings represent people, animals, and other objects that were of significance in the world as people back then experienced it. Those drawings also convey experiences and important meanings; the paintings were the basis for stories or served as messages for others. It is thus safe to assume that what we see here are the beginnings of a developing system of writing.

GRAPHIC REPRESENTATIONS ALWAYS HAVE A MEANING, EVEN WHEN THEY ARE NOTHING MORE THAN A FEW LINES OR SPLOTCHES OF COLOR.

2.11
VISUAL PROCESSING DISORDER (VPD)

Deficits

in fine motor skills and visual processing in
preschool-age children

The visual and graphomotor skills developed in the preschool
years are of utmost importance for learning and working successfully in school later. Many parents tend to underestimate
the significance of practicing graphomotor skills in the preschool years, and unfortunately young boys in particular are
too often given the false reassurance that these skills are not
decisive for their success in school and life. However, this does
not help children overcome impaired coordination in their graphomotor skills, which can have dire consequences once the
children start school.

Kindergartens that offer limited opportunities for children
to practice their fine motor and graphomotor skills through
crafts, drawing, and painting, and have no programs for letting children practice the use of paper and pencils are doing a
poor job of preparing children for school. Children who prefer to
play outdoors, never want to paint, and avoid games in which
they have to follow structured rules often have considerable
developmental deficits in these areas. If these developmental
delays are not identified before the child is enrolled in school,
successful therapy is much more challenging.

CHECKLIST

VISUAL AND MOTOR SKILL
DEFICITS IN PRESCHOOL-AGE CHILDREN.

- ○ Does not like to paint
- ○ Has difficulty coloring within the lines
- ○ Draws only rough sketches, human figures missing details, such as arms or legs
- ○ Cannot draw diagonal lines, such as a triangle
- ○ Prefers to play with interlocking bricks (Duplo, Lego)
- ○ Cannot button up clothing correctly
- ○ Cannot tie shoes
- ○ Is uncertain and anxious when catching balls
- ○ Does not like swinging on a swing set
- ○ Does not like balancing
- ○ Moves very cautiously on downward sloping paths
- ○ Gets car sick
- ○ Has little endurance when looking at picture books with many details
- ○ Does not like playing board games or Memory
- ○ Is not very skilled at putting together jigsaw puzzles
- ○ Appears clumsy, bumps into things, is awkward in pouring liquids, spills food
- ○ Often gets injured because of bumping into things or misjudging distances
- ○ Is uncertain about which hand is dominant, right / left
- ○ Has difficulty distinguishing between right / left
- ○ Has trouble with verbal descriptions of position, such as above, below, right or left
- ○ Shows no interest in symbols, letters or numbers

" If you have put a checkmark next to more than four or five of these statements for your preschooler, a thorough examination of your child's visual development as well as development of gross and fine motor skills is highly recommended. "

check ...

3

Chapter

Neurophysiology
of Vision

3

NEUROPHYSIOLOGY
OF VISION

3.01

WHEN 20/20 VISION IS NOT ENOUGH: TYPICAL SYMPTOMS OF BINOCULAR VISION DISORDERS IN SCHOOL CHILDREN

Vision is a holistic process that involves the eyes, large parts of the brain, and the autonomic nervous system (ANS). When seeing becomes an effort, perceptual disorders can also affect varied parts of the body, causing headaches or stomachaches, dizziness when reading, or nausea. Of course, these symptoms are not unique to children but can also occur in adults. The entire complex of symptoms is called **asthenopia**.

From Laura's story, told below, you will learn what the typical symptoms of functional binocular vision disorders are and how they present themselves in everyday situations. These disorders affect children's ability to learn and concentrate. Similar to to the symptoms of Attention Deficit Disorder or other behavioral disorders, these perceptual difficulties have different causes. Unfortunately, there is not enough awareness of underlying visual factors causing learning and concentration issues. This information is an important missing link for parents and teachers, as millions of schoolchildren are affected.

Laura's struggles in Reading and Spelling

In her first year in school, Laura did not have any learning difficulties. In fact, she learned the letters of the alphabet rather quickly and was soon able to read. She enjoyed writing and liked making up little stories she would then write down. Her parents were a bit frustrated with Laura's "spelling," but the teacher was glad that Laura took so well to the concept of writing through "temporary spelling," also known as phonetic spelling. This child-centered approach to teaching literacy encourages children to start with phonetic spelling, where they are instructed to write the word as it sounds when spoken. Through phonetic spelling, words are rarely spelled correctly. Nonetheless with this method, Laura's teacher recommended that parents do not correct strange spellings such as "matha" for "mother," "vyl" for "will," and "purrheps" for "perhaps." As she explained, this teaching method was designed to encourage children to write and enjoy the process and Laura definitely was having fun writing!

Though Laura was a bit slower than her classmates in learning to read short words, her teacher was not concerned. On Laura's report card at the end of the first school year, the teacher praised the girl's enthusiastic participation in class. The teacher's only criticism was that Laura was a bit slow in her work and was failing at acccurately copying short texts from the board. The teacher's recommendation was that Laura should practice this skill more often.

Observing Laura closely revealed that indeed she worked very slowly and meticulously. For example, when she copied text from the board, she painstakingly wrote each letter into her notebook, and this process took a long time, but even so, what was written in her notebook was riddled with mistakes. Letters were omitted from words, endings of words were left out, and entire words were missing. When copying math problems, Laura also made many mistakes, which naturally led to more mistakes in figuring out the solutions.

Sometimes Laura tried to speed up her copying by not looking at her notebook. She would stare the board and copied the words without looking at her notebook. Of course, that was a bit quicker than copying each letter individually, but because Laura could not see what her writing hand was doing, her writing became illegible, and she would eventually have to give up this method.

Eye Exam finds Perfect Visual Acuity

Laura's teacher observed the girl closely and noticed that Laura was blinking and squinting often while reading and writing. Laura often rubbed her eyes and sometimes even covered one eye with her hand. The teacher suggested that Laura's eyes be examined to see if she needed glasses. However, after thorough examination, the eye doctor found that Laura's visual acuity was perfectly fine and that she definitely did not need glasses.

In second grade, the subject matter she had to learn caused Laura even more problems, and her ability to read or write longer texts deteriorated significantly. When reading and writing or copying text, Laura showed "difficulties concentrating" – at least that's how her work was interpreted. Initially, her writing was neat and free of errors, but by about the middle of the page in her notebook, mistakes began to creep in, and the last half of her page was teeming with errors. Her handwriting, too, became less and less neat toward the bottom of the page, and it looked as though Laura had simply lost interest in her work after only a short time or as if she was not sufficiently concentrating on what she was doing.

Laura had similar problems with reading. She did well with the first and second sentence and read them fluently, but after that she made more and more mistakes, confusing letters, leaving out endings, and finally even guessing words rather than reading them. When she guessed wrong and the text then made no sense, she didn't seem to notice. As a result, Laura's reading comprehension was not very good.

At home, Laura tried with all sorts of excuses to avoid doing the reading exercises her teacher had recommended. Only with great effort Laura's mother could get her daughter to practice reading with her. Moreover, neither Laura and her mother could see any improvement in Laura's reading as a result of the exercises, nor could the teacher. Even though Laura had been enthusiastic about learning to read in first grade, by second grade she no longer enjoyed it at all.

Laura Struggles to Apply Spelling Rules

By the time Laura was in third grade, her problems at school had become much worse. Teachers now expected third graders to follow and apply spelling rules. Only a small percentage of words at that level are spelled phonetically, and Laura could really no longer rely on the phonetic method she had been allowed to use in first and second grade. Laura found herself in the situation where she had gone through two years of learning and memorizing the phonetic, and thus incorrect spelling of words.

Since Laura could not develop the reading skills allowing her to access texts easily, an important source of knowledge and tool for learning about spelling and other subjects remained unavailable to her. In books we can see words spelled correctly, and all we have to do is look at them, read, and memorize them. **Reading is an essential skill for learning how to spell.** The other children in Laura's class had a much easier time letting go of "temporary" or phonetic spelling than Laura. They were also able to better adapt as the teacher now graded the children's dictation exercises. Laura took a very long time to learn and memorize the spelling of words that demonstrate spelling rules for certain sound or letter combinations. During dictation exercises, the teachers's pace was too fast. Laura and her grades suffered, as a result she would usually get an F or E.

BEECH   BITSH   BEACH

          BEETSH   BITCH

BAECH   BETCH

When she was in doubt about how to spell a word, Laura still resorted to phonetic spelling – just as she had learned to do in first and second grade. She could not completely let go of this way of writing, and since correct English spelling is hardly ever based on how a word sounds, Laura had serious spelling problems starting in third grade. As a result of all these problems, her self-confidence had been seriously impaired, and she became very anxious before each dictation exercise. Moreover, Laura didn't want to practice reading with her mother anymore because all the practicing seemed to have no effect.

DICTATION PRACTICE

> Praktise Dicktation
>
> We are havin a party for
> mi birday today. My blrthda' is
> to dai dut mi party was
> yestaday. I've invited all my frends
> from scool to com. We are
> going to watsh a movi and
> make our own podcorn

Snoopy

Frustrated with Reading

Soon, Laura was reading only when her parents forced her to do it. Even though her mother regularly took Laura to bookstores and bought her every book Laura showed the slightest interest in, the girl's reading behavior remained unchanged. She would begin reading a book with great enthusiasm and tell her parents she'd definitely finish this book, but after reading a few pages, Laura would put it aside and set it on top of the stack of other books she had started and not finished. She began complaining of headaches when she came home from school, became short-tempered and was clearly exhausted. Reminders that she had to do her homework brought on a new attack of headache, and if her mother then allowed Laura to take a break, the girl played cheerfully in the garden and the headache was no longer an issue. Laura's mother got the impression that the girl's headaches were not real but served only as an excuse not to do homework.

Neither a thorough examination by the pediatrician, that involved blood tests, nor an exam by the pediatric neurologist, including an EEG, showed any evidence of illness. Laura's parents considered consulting an educational guidance counselor. They hoped that family therapy might help them resolve the conflicts and issues regarding Laura's work attitudes and habits.

When Visual Acuity Is Not the Problem

All the symptoms described above have one common cause; and that cause is not deficient visual acuity.

The eye doctor checked Laura's visual acuity at a distance of 20 feet, and Laura had to read the smallest line of letters and numbers with each eye separately. Since she could do this without any problem, Laura's visual acuity was determined 20/20 and perfectly fine. However, the ophthalmologist did not check Laura's acuity at reading distance and did not examine any special functions of binocular vision. The comprehensive exam of binocular functions conducted later by a developmental optometrist showed that Laura's binocular vision was significantly impaired.

Although Laura had excellent visual acuity in each eye separately and could read letters and numbers at a distance of 20 feet, close up she simply could not see clearly with both eyes together. She was diagnosed with a dysfunction in accommodative flexibility and convergence insufficiency with intermittent central suppression. She had no stable and robust amplitude of fusion and showed significant deficits in 3D perception; moreover, her ability to move her eyes horizontally, which is necessary for fluent reading, was like that of five-year-old preschooler.

To help you understand the technical terms mentioned above, the next section further discusses the neuroanatomy and neurophysiology of vision as brain functions that are crucial for stress-free learning and concentration.

You will read about the embryonic development of the eyes, binocular vision (seeing with both eyes), and the anatomical brain structures processing visual information. Along the way, you will learn about eye movements, about the cranial nerves involved in the process of seeing, and about the interactions between vision and other functions of the body.

3.02
PERFECT VISION IS TEAMWORK: SEEING WITH BOTH EYES

If we had only one eye – as some mythical creatures are said to have – we would have a lot of brain volume and processing power available for other tasks. However, because we have two eyes, vast areas of our brain are dedicated to the work of constantly and perfectly adjusting the position of two "precision cameras" – namely, our two open eyes. The brain makes sure that at every distance and at any time, whether we steadily look at something with our eyes or move them quickly from one thing to another, both eyes are always looking at the same point – and this adjustment is absolutely precise to the millimeter.

Adjusting the autofocus of the two eyes, practically at lightning speed, to every possible viewing distance is a very complicated task. This adjustment is essential to seeing clearly at all times and allows us to organize our spatial perception so that we can rely on it for our body's motor functions. After all, our eyes allow us to navigate and maneuver our own body, cars, planes, tennis rackets, and writing instruments in the way and direction we wish. To achieve this end, our neurons must perform complex feats of organization. In particular, binocular vision requires complicated neuronal organizational structures that reorganize themselves repeatedly in sensorimotor feedback loops.

Sensorimotor feedback here refers to the fact that perception and movement of eyes and body are at all times working together in a coordinated way. Just imagine the complex task your eyes carry out when you want to hit a rapidly approaching tennis ball with your racket. The slightest changes in the tennis ball's trajectory must be perceived by your eyes. By rapidly moving both eyes into the appropriate perceptual position, you perceive the ball and can track it as a moving object. At the same time your 3D perception is functioning with great precision even when objects move very fast; and with the help of this visual information you can guide the movements of your arm muscles so precisely that you hit the ball just right. This is a highly complex and complicated achievement and our brain has developed biologically in order to provide the vast amount of energy, capacity, and processing power, needed for tasks just described.

3.03
EMBRYONIC DEVELOPMENT OF THE EYES

From the earliest stages of embryonic development our eyes are part of the brain, called the cerebrum, the anterior and largest part of the human brain. Before we can even see any brain in the embryo, the eyes begin to form, initially as two small vesicles, one on the left and one on the right. Then bulge out from the bubble-shaped mass of cells that will later develop into the embryo's brain. The retina begins to develop from the skin of these vesicles, and later gives rise to the development of the transparent, light-sensitive receptor cells that will eventually be interconnected with each other. This complex network of photoreceptor cells makes it possible for the first phase of visual information processing to take place right within the eyes. In other words, the retina, the eyes' initial information processing system, is formed long before the eyes themselves are complete.

The eye vesicles then invaginate, turn themselves inward, towards the optic cup, and in that process push the transparent photoreceptors towards the back of the eyes, the area called the ocular fundus. There, the photoreceptors become embedded in the ink-black tissues of the choroid, which is a layer of tissue rich in blood vessels that does not reflect any light at all. At this point in the embryo's development, the receptors are functionally shielded and fully embedded. They prepare for the reception of light coming in only from the front, where the pupil of the eye will develop later. However, before that happens, a drop-shaped bit of material sinks down from the tissues that will later become the eye's outer layer into the optic cup that has formed in the meantime. Here, this material is enclosed and will later develop into the lens of the eye.

The optic cup eventually closes to form the eye ball, remains connected with the brain throughout all developmental phases by a kind of stalk. This structure later becomes the optic nerve and develops inside the brain into the visual pathway.

In the next developmental step after the eyes have attained their spherical shape, six extraocular muscles develop on each eye, four of them are rectus muscles, controlling movement up and down and left and right, and two are oblique muscles, rotating the eyes inward and outward. Several cranial nerves are needed to coordinate and control the movements of these extraocular muscles.

3.04
FROM PIXELS TO PICTURES: THE VISUAL PATHWAY

When we open our eyes, we expect to see the world around us at a glance – the world with all the things and creatures in it, all the shapes, colors, and details. We expect this as a baseline and rarely, if ever, think about the mechanics that make it possible. Seeing happens so very quickly that we don't notice the many individual components that make up our rapid and fully integrated visual perceptions.

You may remember from high school Physics classes that light is extremely fast electromagnetic radiation, for light travels through space at a speed of 186,000 miles per second before it arrives in our eyes. Perhaps you still remember the experiment with the pinhole camera from your physics classes? That experiment demonstrated that the pictures our retina receives are upside down. That follows logically from the laws of Physics. However, our sense of vision cannot really be compared to a simple pinhole camera. Rather, what is crucial for our eyesight is the "software" that receives, processes, and stores visual information.

The retina is a part of the brain, but located just outside of it. Its task is to capture streams of colored light and black-and-white contrasts in a network of dot-shaped receptors. This network of receptors is organized into a sort of system of coordinates that allows us to pinpoint the location of objects we see. However, the retina itself does not yet give us pictures of shapes, figures contours, lines, or contrasts, and even motion is not perceived until a later stage in the process of seeing. For the processes of perception following the initial activity of the retinal receptor cells, numerous learning processes are required. For example, we – or rather our brain – must learn through experience, which combinations of characteristics regularly occur at the same time at the same location, and can thus be expected. In other words, seeing is a learned brain function. Recognizing and naming what we see is possible because our sense of sight is connected with other regions of the brain.

How visual information is transported along the visual pathway, how it is analyzed and segmented into individual components, and how transport paths and steps of information processing are made available is a very complicated field of neurobiology. Countless scientists all over the world – including several Nobel laureates – are working on understanding how we see. Their research helps us to know more about the processing of visual information and understand certain illnesses. Forthcoming research aims at the development of an artificial retina chip that would restore sight to people who have become blind.

→　**Below you will find an abbreviated description of the components and interconnections of our visual pathway.**

Transportation of Light Information

When we look at something, we see either the light source itself or the objects it illuminates. The **retina** in our eye processes this light information with the help of highly specialized **light receptor cells** also called photoreceptors. With the photosensitive protein molecules they contain, these cells turn light – electromagnetic waves – into chemical and electrical signals, thus converting this information into a form that can be transported by the nervous system. In this process, light that falls upon the retina is transformed into activation states of retinal cells.

For a clearer description of how images are processed by our sense of sight, we can use the concept of pixel. It's a model for the smallest elementary particles of digital image processing.

At the level of retina receptors, we have nothing more than a mosaic of individual, pixel-like states of excitation that are bundled together into so-called **receptive fields** and are either switched **ON** or **OFF**. Our visual perception is based on points of light that are constantly active and changing in both space and time. You can picture your retina and the areas of the brain where the primary visual information is processed as an electronic display or score board, much like the ones seen at airports and on billboards. **Countless points of light captured by receptors that are active or passive at different moments in time organize and reorganize themselves into various patterns in just milliseconds.**

The retina has two types of **receptor cells**, that serve very different functions. The so-called **rods** are highly sensitive to light and specialized to respond to **light-dark contrasts** and **motion**. They enable us to see the contours of objects and their movements even in twilight and at low light intensity. "All cats are gray in the dark," as the saying goes. This refers to how in twilight or at night we can see only shades of gray. In daylight, however, the activity of these retinal receptor cells enables us to perceive motion. The rod cells do not give us a colored and certainly not a clear, sharp picture.

Providing such a clear picture is the function of the so-called **cones**. These cells are not particularly light-sensitive, but they respond to **colors** and **contrasts**. They are distributed across the retina in such a way that very precise and sharp vision becomes possible. In particular, these cells respond differently to differently colored light. For example, one type of cone cell reacts to shortwave light which corresponds to the color **blue**. A second type of cone cell is specialized for perceiving light of medium wavelength, that is **green** and related colors. A third type of cone cell serves as a sort of antenna, perceiving longwave light, which we perceive as **red**. Mixed colors, such as orange or turquoise, are the result of one color activating several receptor cells, each to a different degree.

In addition to 120 million rod cells that are evenly distributed across the entire retina, we have 6 million cone cells, most of which are located in the center of the retina where they form the **fovea centralis**, the area where our vision is sharpest. In this area of the retina, the light receptors are positioned in such a way that they are not covered by the layer of retinal ganglion cells which would otherwise slightly dim the amount of light coming in. However, the transformation of a light pattern on the retina into electric nerve signals is only the beginning of the process of seeing. To process the visual information we have received and react to it with as little delay as possible, the **visual pathway** serves as a sort of high-speed conduit that conducts information from the eyes to the brain. The visual pathway is a superfast conduit that bundles and crosses fibers carrying visual information and then distributes them widely to the vision centers in the brain through the optic radiation, a collection of nerve cell axons carrying visual information to the visual cortex.

The Essentials in Brief

→ The **optic nerve** (Latin name: nervus opticus) consists of about one million bundled afferent retinal cell fibers, conducting impulses from the eyes to the brain. This nerve is essentially like a complex fiber optic cable with a diameter of up to 0.2 inches. It exits toward the brain at the back of the eye; and this is what creates our blind spot there.

→ Signals are then transported from the retina all the way to the occipital lobe at the back of the head, and there the signals are received for further processing in the outer layer of the brain, the primary visual cortex.

→ The **visual pathway** transports visual signals to the brain at lightning speed. From encoding of the image on the retina to the first measurable impulses in the primary visual cortex this takes less than 10 milliseconds.

→ The optic nerves of the right and left eye meet about 2 inches behind the eyeball in the **optic chiasm**, an x-shaped structure formed by the crossing of the optic nerves. Half of the fibers of each of the two nerve bundles change sides here, so that half of the signals from the left eye are processed in the right hemisphere of the brain and vice versa.

→ Only the fibers coming from **fovea centralis** are crossed **and** uncrossed on their path to the brain. Thus the information they carry is **represented in both hemispheres simultaneously**.

→ This superfast transport of information is possible because there is only one switching station between the retina and the primary visual cortex. This station is called the **lateral geniculate nucleus (LGN)**. Most of the fibers of the visual pathway are switched over here and run from here to the cerebral cortex.

→ About 10 percent of the fibers branch off at the lateral geniculate nucleus and form a connecting path leading to **unconscious areas of seeing**. This part of the visual pathway provides very important **connections to the balancing or vestibular system** as well as a connection to the hypothalamus. The hypothalamus informs our **"inner clock"** about light conditions and also regulates our **unconscious eye movements** as they track moving objects automatically. In addition, at this "junction box" a kind of feedback is generated that regulates how much light falls on the retina by adjusting the **dilation of the pupils**.

→ The **optic radiation** forms the last segment of the visual pathway and fans out broadly and branches extensively before it reaches the visual cortex, the visual area of the cerebral cortex at the rear pole of the cerebrum.

→ The information streaming in from **136 million retinal receptors** is then processed by more than **500 million nerve cells** or neurons in the cerebral cortex.

→ **The primary visual cortex, also called the striate area (so named for its distinctive stripes), works very precisely with a map for pixels.**

→ One of the key elements of this area's high level of precision is the **spatial organization of information**, the so-called **retinotopic organization**. This means that photoreceptor cells that are adjacent to each other on the retina are represented in the visual cortex with great precision. Thus, a sort of map is created that allows us to pinpoint the location of objects in space.

→ This map, however, is greatly distorted because the information from the fovea centralis is represented disproportionately. After all, every precise fixation of our eyes and every close look happens with the

CUBE-SHAPED SECTION, DETAIL OF THE STRIATE AREA

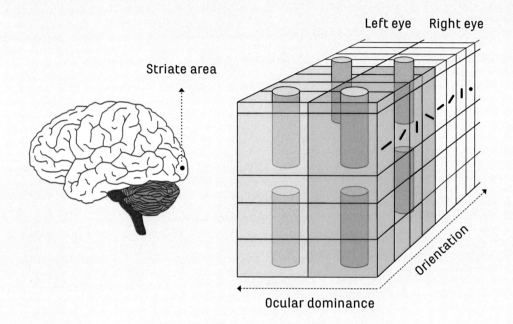

Striate area

Left eye   Right eye

Orientation

Ocular dominance

fovea. The fovea's location is at the center of the retina, forming the area where we see with maximum precision. In this area the retina has the best visual acuity, and the striate area has a **particularly high capacity for processing very sharp images**.

→ **About 80 percent of the primary visual cortex is dedicated to impulses from the fovea, which itself measures less than 0.04 inches.** The enormous focus on the fovea makes sense in terms of function. If the entire retina offered the same sharp images as the fovea, we would need an optic nerve with the diameter of an elephant trunk.

→ The **striate area** works with extraordinary precision thanks to its highly specialized cells.

→ The actual analysis of what was seen begins only in the visual cortex, more precisely, in the layer of the striate area ("striped area") that is called **V1**.

→ In the striate area only very specialized stimuli are processed, and in terms of neuroanatomy, we find here the utmost order and precision. For example, the cell layers are stacked in closely adjacent "blocks" of cells, with those coming from the **left** eye's visual impressions alternating with the ones coming from the **right** eye's impressions (so-called **ocular dominance columns, ODC**).

→ Each of these blocks contains **orientation stripes** that are exclusively specialized for **perceiving orientation or direction of lines**. One orientation stripe can perceive only lines angled 45 degrees; the other one only those that are angled 90 degrees. Neither can perceive any other orientations. All possible **tilt angles between 0 and 180 degrees** are distributed like this and are covered in gradation steps of 10 degrees each. Each of them is processed in strictly separated but adjacent areas.

→ There are other specialized areas that are dedicated to process perception of **light spots, edges**, dark-light **contrasts**, or **curved lines**.

Translation ▪ Eating

The eight standard strokes of Chinese calligraphy

→ It has only been a few decades since knowledge about the function of these specialized cells in our visual cortex has become available to us. In **1981** David Hubel, an American scientist, and Torsten Wiesel from Sweden were awarded the **Nobel Prize** for physiology and medicine for their discoveries about **"information processing in the visual system."**

→ However, much earlier, in fact more than 5,000 years ago, people in China developed the **eight standard lines of calligraphy** ("beautiful handwriting"). Very likely those Chinese characters are the oldest known elements of an abstract writing system. **What is especially interesting about these basic calligraphy lines is that they are astonishingly similar to the spatial specialization of the orientation stripes in the primary visual cortex** (see picture on p. 125, Schuhmacher, H. 2006).

→ In addition to the primary visual cortex (V1), which conducts a precise analysis of shape components – like **lines, spots, edges, and curved lines** – there are about two dozen other areas in the cerebral cortex dedicated to a more complex analysis of the visual world. Images are then analyzed in other brain regions located further downstream, such as the parietal lobe and the temporal lobe. Of particular importance are two branchings of the visual pathway.

THE VISUAL PATHWAYS

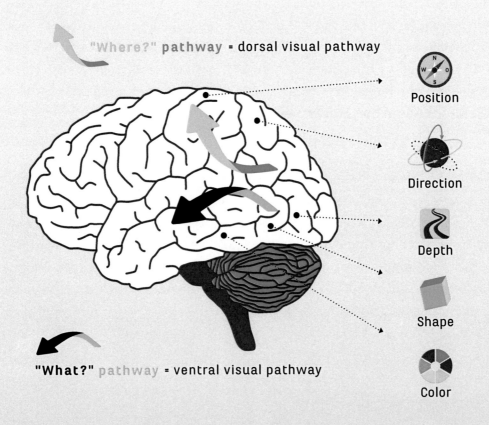

"Where?" pathway = dorsal visual pathway

Position

Direction

Depth

Shape

Color

"What?" pathway = ventral visual pathway

→ The upper or **dorsal visual pathway** runs to the parietal lobe or parietal cortex. This pathway is also called the **"where" path** because it is dedicated to answering the question of **"where something is located?"**. It analyzes object positions in relation to the viewer as well as the direction of motion and is involved in planning the body's movements in relation to an object seen. Simple movements of our body in space, like reaching for an apple, as well as complex motor activities, such as hitting back a tennis ball approaching at lightning speed, make use of this system.

→ The lower or **ventral visual pathway** runs toward the temporal lobe or the temporal cortex. It is also called the **"what" pathway** because its function is to answer the question **"what is this?"**. It serves to identify, recognize, and name objects we see, while also analyzing their size, shape, and color. For example, when you look at a blue letter in the illustration, your brain grasps the letter's color, shape, and size and its position in relation to the other letters and the illustration as a whole, all at the same time. In addition, your sense of sight informs you that, depending on which way you hold the book, there is an illustration in vertical orientation that includes both writing and images with an image at its center and writing arranged above, below, and next to an image of a cerebrum presented in profile view. Here your sense of sight has grasped and processed all this information within milliseconds. If you were trying to describe all this information into words, you would need much, much more time.

3.05
HOW THE EYES MOVE

Our eyes are round, ball-shaped, and cushioned in their bony eye sockets by a bit of fatty tissue. Thanks to their shape, positioning, and the six muscles on which the eye ball is suspended, our eyes can execute soft gliding and highly precise movements. To coordinate their joint movement properly, both eye balls must always move at the same time. Every eye movement consists of an impulse that is coordinated by twelve muscles working at the same time. Even simple right-to-left movements of the eyes require simultaneous activity of all ocular muscles.

We can move our eyes horizontally and vertically and can also rotate them, but nearly all eye movements are combinations of these movement patterns. When you are reading a text message on your smartphone, a story on your tablet or in your book, or writing in a notebook, when you are reading, texting or writing, you are always looking slightly downward and moving your eyes horizontally from left to right as well as in a diagonal vertical movement that allows you to move on to the next line.

Our entire motor system is organized **antagonistically**. That means that every action of our muscles involves an **agonist** and an **antagonist**. When both muscles work at the same time and equally strongly, then stability is possible. If movement is called for, then the muscle activity has to be coordinated and synchronized. **When one muscle tenses, its antagonist must relax sufficiently at the same time so that the movement can occur.** For example, when you want to lift something with your arm and bend your forearm for this purpose, your biceps muscle tenses. At the same time, its antagonist, the triceps muscle, must relax in order to allow the movement of your forearm.

The same principle applies to our eyes. However, here, two "balls" must be moved by twelve muscles working at the same time. If our eyes move in the same direction, for example, when we look to the lower left, a total of twelve muscles must work at the same time. Some of them will shorten by tensing or flexing and others will at the same time lengthen by relaxing, and they will do this at very high speed. After each movement, they are immediately ready for the next one as we change the direction of our gaze.

Our external eye muscles constantly receive impulses from three large brain nerves that are always active, even when we are sleeping. Every eye muscle is innervated by about 1,000 so-called motor neurons. These neurons branch out, spreading throughout each muscle, and each branch then provides nerve impulses to between four and ten muscle fibers. This unit of muscle fiber and nerve fiber is called a **motor unit**. The tensile force of a muscle is enhanced thanks to the activation of motor units that had previously been inactive or had not been used to full capacity. The frequency of electric discharges the motor neurons send into motor units can get as high as 300 impulses per second.

THE SIX EXTERNAL EYE MUSCLES

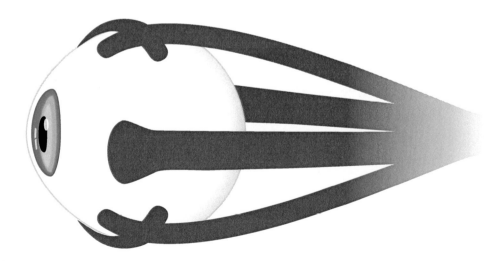

The more subtle and precise a muscle movement has to be, the fewer muscle fibers each nerve fiber has to supply with impulses. The ratio of the connections between muscle fibers to impulse-providing nerve fibers varies widely. For example, in the eye muscles one motor unit may consist of four to ten muscle fibers. That means that **one nerve impulse supplies four to ten muscle fibers**. In larger muscles, the skeletal muscles of our spine or legs for instance, precise control of micro-movements is not entailed, motor units consist of up to 2,000 muscle fibers. In these muscles **one nerve impulse is sufficient to set 2,000 large muscle fibers** in motion.

Once we open our eyes, they remain constantly in motion. During the so-called fixations, when our eyes are fixed on what we are looking at, visual information is consciously perceived and processed. The rapid movements of the eyes from one fixation to the next are called saccades (from the Latin term for abrupt, jerky movements). A **gaze saccade** then is a very rapid movement of both eyes as they navigate to another point of fixation. Saccades can also be described as **ballistic movements**, which means that once a saccade is underway, the movement cannot be corrected or adjusted while it is in process. Indeed, in the brief moment of jumping rapidly from one gaze saccade to the next, our eyes are not taking in any information but are "blind." Saccades can reach angular velocities of **1,000 degrees per second**; their amplitudes range from 60 degrees to a maximum of 600 degrees, and each saccade lasting between **30 to 100 milliseconds**.

Looking at an object in the close-up range requires opposing movements of the eyes. **The axes of both eyes turn inward, toward each other, in convergence movement.** At the same time, the accommodation-convergence reflex adjusts the sharpness of the image to the viewing distance. Of course, this description of eye movements applies only to steady fixation on a point. If other visual functions are called for at the same time, the coordination of the eye muscles becomes even more complicated. For example, for reading or writing our eyes must consistently move horizontally and also vertically as we advance from one line to the next. Throughout these movements, our eyes must maintain the basic **convergence position of their axes** reliably and consistently.

3.06
VISION AND THE 12 CRANIAL NERVES

We are often talking about our five senses and refer with this term to our entire perceptual system. However, a closer look at our anatomy and brain physiology shows that these five senses are actually part of a larger system. Anatomically speaking, we have 12 cranial nerves that make up our entire perceptual system.

The cranial nerves originate from specialized core areas of the brain and are visible on the underside of the cerebrum as large bundles of nerve fibers. In pictures, these nerves are numbered in sequence from front to back with Roman numerals. Today, there is consensus that cranial nerve I, the **olfactory nerve**, and **cranial nerve II, the optic nerve, are not nerves in the strict sense but rather are part of the cerebrum located just outside the brain**.

Four of our five large senses – seeing, hearing, smelling, and tasting – are located in the head area. Only the sense of touch and our awareness for our own body movements, the so-called proprioception, as well as the autonomic nervous system (ANS) are distributed throughout our body.

The cranial nerves thus are large bundles of nerves that connect our sensory organs with their corresponding centers in the brain. They are organized by function and can be subdivided into several groups. The large nerves dedicated

THE XII CRANIAL NERVES

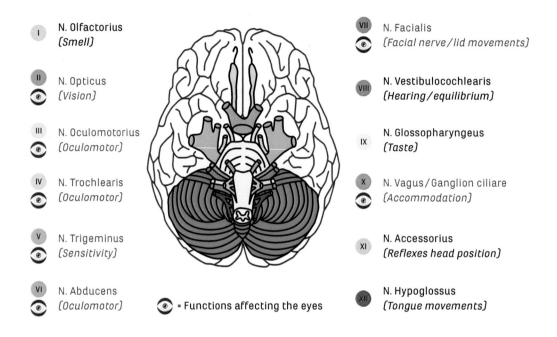

I — N. Olfactorius
(Smell)

II — N. Opticus
(Vision)

III — N. Oculomotorius
(Oculomotor)

IV — N. Trochlearis
(Oculomotor)

V — N. Trigeminus
(Sensitivity)

VI — N. Abducens
(Oculomotor)

VII — N. Facialis
(Facial nerve/lid movements)

VIII — N. Vestibulocochlearis
(Hearing/equilibrium)

IX — N. Glossopharyngeus
(Taste)

X — N. Vagus/Ganglion ciliare
(Accommodation)

XI — N. Accessorius
(Reflexes head position)

XII — N. Hypoglossus
(Tongue movements)

= Functions affecting the eyes

exclusively to sensory perception include the olfactory nerve or cranial nerve I **(Latin name: nervus olfactorius)**, the optic nerve or cranial nerve II **(nervus opticus)**, cranial nerve V **(nervus trigeminus)**, which organizes the sensitivity of the head area, and cranial nerve VIII **(nervus vestibulochlearis)**, a large nerve that connects hearing and the vestibular system, our balance and equilibrium.

Another group of cranial nerves is dedicated exclusively to motor functions. For example, cranial nerve VII **(nervus facialis)** controls our facial expressions, like our facial muscles and the movements of the eyelids. Cranial nerve XI **(nervus accessorius)** controls our neck musculature and the reflexes governing head position, which in turn regulate the positioning of the sensory organs in the head. Cranial nerve XII **(nervus hypoglossus)** controls the tongue muscles and thus makes speaking possible.

Three of the 12 cranial nerves – cranial nerve III **(nervus oculomotorius)**, nerve IV **(nervus trochlearis)**, and nerve VI **(nervus abducens)** – together have only one function: controlling the musculature of the eyes.

Another noteworthy cranial nerve is nerve X **(nervus vagus)**; it organizes the parasympathetic portion of our vast autonomic nervous system that extends throughout our entire body. This nerve provides the impulses for the organs in throat, chest, and belly and for this purpose, forms local webs of nerves, best known as the solar plexus.

Moreover, cranial nerve X, the vagus nerve, is important for our conscious sensory perception and especially for the quality of the images we see. One branch of the vagus nerve runs to the eye and there regulates the muscle tone of the ciliary muscles, responsible for the curvature of the lens and for the autofocus function of our eyes. This nerve is also involved in the **accommodation-convergence reflex** moving the axes of our eyes into the appropriate convergent perceptual position, and for that purpose it is closely interconnected with cranial nerves III, IV, and VI, which control the movements of the eye muscles.

While only one nerve bundle, namely, cranial nerve VIII (nervus vestibulochlearis), governs all functions of hearing and equilibrium, **seven of the twelve cranial nerves have a direct influence on visual perception**. Even cranial nerve number VIII, which is primarily for hearing and balance, is involved with the integration between the visual and vestibular system that helps our body maintain itself upright. In other words, our brain's neuronatomy shows an enormous neuronal investment in the complex process of vision.

3.07
VISION AND THE AUTONOMIC NERVOUS SYSTEM

The autonomic nervous system is part of the peripheral and central nervous system and governs the communication between organs. It consists of the **sympathetic** and the **parasympathetic nervous system** and is thus organized in a dualistic and antagonistic way. The functions of our body are held in balance by two large systems providing impulses and working in opposition to each other. The autonomic nervous system controls our unconscious bodily functions and is only to a very limited extent subject to our intentional control. This system is a primeval component of our nervous system, and by means of unconscious, lightning-fast, and intelligent reflex mechanisms it regulates vital functions of the body and our organs, thus ensuring the survival of our species.

You can picture the **sympathetic nervous system (SNS)** as working much like the gas pedal in your car. By releasing the **stress hormone adrenaline**, the SNS prepares our body to fight or rapidly flee from danger. If any danger – even an imagined one – threatens us, the sympathetic nervous system increases our muscle tension and the blood flow to the muscles so that we can quickly run away or – if that is no longer possible – get ready to fight. For example, our breathing rate and blood pressure are immediately elevated to ensure that we have as much oxygen as possible while we are running for our life. Since digestion is not important in dangerous situations, the organs in our abdomen receive only reduced blood flow during this time of high alert.

When we are running for our life, seeing at great distance is very important. Our pupils dilate when we are on alert to allow better peripheral vision and a more comprehensive view of our surroundings. At the same time our visual acuity in the close-up range is reduced, and our eyes are ready for seeing at greater distances. After all, when we are running as fast as we can to save ourselves, we must be able to see what's in the far distance and have an overview of the larger terrain. The excellent visual acuity we need when reading leisurely in our rocking chair is not needed in such danger situations when our body tells us "it's a matter of life or death" and prepares all functions in the best possible way for survival.

The **parasympathetic nervous system (PNS)** is the antagonist of the sympathetic nervous system and serves the opposite function. The parasympathetic nervous system even has its own cranial nerve. If we keep the image of the sympathetic nervous system as working like a gas pedal, then we can think of the parasympathetic nervous system as functioning much like a

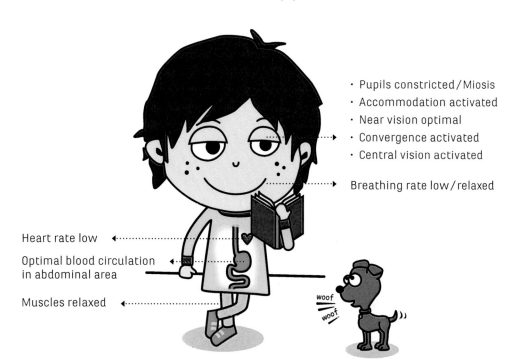

Parasympathetic Nervous System

Relaxation, enjoyment

· Pupils constricted / Miosis
· Accommodation activated
· Near vision optimal
· Convergence activated
· Central vision activated

Breathing rate low / relaxed

Heart rate low

Optimal blood circulation
in abdominal area

Muscles relaxed

woof
woof

brake. The parasympathetic nervous system has a soothing and calming influence.It slows down our heart rate and lowers our blood pressure and breathing rate. By way of the **solar plexus** the organs in our abdomen are well supplied with blood, and the processes of digestion are well supported. The parasympathetic nervous system is of great importance for regulating stress because it relaxes all muscles throughout our body.

As long as no danger is imminent, we can be relaxed and thus also take an interest in what is happening around us. For example, in our relaxed state, we may prepare a meal, build or craft something with our hands, draw, sew, read, or write. To engage in these activities, we must be able to see well at close range. Accordingly, the vagus nerve, which governs the parasympathetic nervous system, is also connected to the eyes: it participates in orienting the eyes to near vision, that is, in activating the accommodation-convergence reflex. The vagus nerve ensures that we see sharp images in near vision and supports our central visual acuity with added depth of focus by reducing the size of the pupil opening.It slows down our heart rate and lowers our blood pressure and breathing rate. By way of the **solar plexus** the organs in our abdomen are well supplied with blood, and the processes of digestion are well supported. The parasympathetic nervous system is of great importance for regulating stress because it relaxes all muscles throughout our body.

MALADAPTIVE
STRESS
CAUSES POOR VISION

By and large, our prehistoric ancestors were well adapted to their life thanks mainly to the autonomic nervous system with its antagonistic equilibrium. Unfortunately, in our modern age a new danger has cropped up – we call it stress. Indeed, all kinds of stress affect the quality of our vision. We experience stress not so much in response to real bodily threats like the ones our ancestors faced from wild animals or attacking enemies. Our stress response is triggered for the most part by mere thoughts and emotions. For example, when we feel threatened or afraid before an important test in school, such as a **vocabulary or Math test** or even only before a **dictation exercise in elementary school**, our body steps on the gas pedal, so to speak, thus triggering the corresponding **physiological flight response**. In these times of perceived threat our autonomic nervous system does not want us to attend to tasks that must be done in near vision range. After all, when we are fleeing for our life, solving math problems is not a priority. Instead, our body – that is, the sympathetic nervous system – wants to have a clearer distance view and wants to redirect our attention to the periphery of our visual field so we can see any additional threats that might emerge there.

PHYSIOLOGICAL
RESPONSES
TO STRESS

As you can imagine, children who are afraid of a Math test then sitting at their desk, their heart racing and palms sweating. They are not allowed to move or run away even though their muscles are tensed and ready for flight or action.

Children who are sensitive to visual irritations may suddenly have poor vision. To their eyes, the writing on the math test sheet is blurry and unclear. They cannot see the instructions or questions clearly and thus cannot read them and become even more anxious. At the same time, the other component of the autonomic nervous system, that is, the parasympathetic nervous system, is trying to activate the brake. After all, the flight response, which is governed by the sympathetic nervous system, is entirely useless in the test situation.

As you can see, there is a conflict being fought out in the body of these children, a contest between the gas pedal and the brake. When the children's parasympathetic nervous system, the solar plexus, is activated excessively, the resulting changes in blood flow to the abdominal organs can cause stomachaches. **Children whose visual functions are not stable and who suffer from fear of failure then develop not only vision-related headaches but also stomachaches and nausea.** These physiological reactions are natural and understandable. This is not a case of children faking these symptoms to avoid having to learn and do their school work.

Regarding the eyes, the stress response causes **dilation of the pupils, blurry vision, and convergence insufficiency**. In other words, activating the stress response governed by the sympathetic nervous system always leads to dilation of the pupils. Therefore, as a parent or teacher, when you see that a child has dilated pupils while reading, you can tell that this child is afraid and is working in the physiological mode that has not adapted and the **wrong visual mode** for reading. The relaxed eye position for near vision is always accompanied by undilated pupils. Regular size or smaller pupils can also provide a better range of focus for near vision tasks.

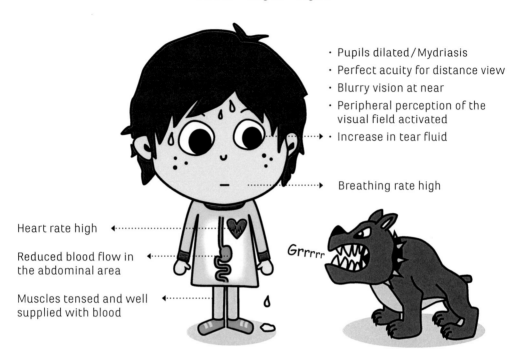

Children affected by the above-described symptoms often say that they **"hate reading"** and now we can better understand why. These kids cannot imagine how anyone could relax in the evening by reading a book or why anyone would want to take books along on a vacation in order to enter an imagined, different, and interesting world through reading.

FORCED TO READ, THE CHILD'S ENTIRE BODY SWITCHES TO STRESS MODE

3.08
PERFECT VISION AT ANY DISTANCE:
THE ACCOMMODATION-CONVERGENCE-REFLEX

To be able to read, you need to have stable convergence as your eyes look down at the text, and you need to have perfect visual acuity and must be able to carry out uniform horizontal reading saccades with both eyes simultaneously. As mentioned above, in this process the **vagus nerve** regulates the pupil diameter and the tone of the ciliary muscles. These in turn control the curvature of the lens and the **autofocus function**, the adjustment of the image sharpness to your distance from the object you are looking at. To bring the axes of both eyes into the appropriate position for convergent perception at the same time, the vagus nerve is closely connected to the core areas of the cranial nerves III, IV, and VI, which govern the actions of the 12 external eye muscles.

Now, imagine you are copying something from the blackboard into your notebook; your distance to the notebook is about 16 inches while the distance to the board is about 20 feet. Clearly, you have to adjust sharpness of image as well as convergence and divergence movements to the rapid shifts between these distances. All these movements and adjustments must be perfectly coordinated. Looking at the notebook also involves looking slightly downward, and looking at the board means having to look up, and therefore all 12 eye muscles must work at the same time at top speed and at full capacity for you to be able to carry out these movements in rapid sequence and with the necessary precision.

The complex activity just described involves the **accommodation-conver-gence reflex**, which is a combined reflex. All the components of this reflex are coordinated and synchronized automatically and with great precision to work together at the same time. For example, if the axes of our eyes converge even just slightly, the accommodation reflex is triggered immediately and automatically. Conversely, even the slightest accommodation impulse immediately triggers a small convergence movement. There is no other physiological alternative. In other words, if our eyes move ever so slightly inward, the lens in both eyes is immediately and automatically adjusted in such a way that we can still see clearly.

This reflex is a binocular activity in which all impulses are sent at the same level of intensity to both eyes simultaneously. In contrast, in chickens, for example, the accommodation reflex works for each eye separately. As a result, chickens can see the tiniest grain sharply and accurately, but only with one eye at a time. In the meantime, the other eye can scan the surroundings for potential threats. We do not have that option; we cannot make the image received by one eye a bit sharper than the one received by the other eye. When a person suffers from **anisometropia**, the refractive power of one eye is slightly different from that of the other eye. For example if for the right eye a corrective lens with +3.0 diopters is needed and on the left eye one with only +0.75 diopters, people can have serious problems with accommodation and fusion. Children suffering from such refraction errors need precisely adjusted glasses at the start of Vision Therapy.

3.09
THE RETINA'S CENTER CONTROLS ACUITY AND EYE MOVEMENTS

Clearly, organizing a sensorimotor process as complicated as the movement of the eyes requires an excellent control system. This crucial **control element** is located in the center of the retina of each eye. When we look at the background of the eye, this is where we see the the **macula lutea**, which has a tiny recess or dent, called **fovea centralis**.

This tiny area, which is about the size of the tip of a sewing needle, is the only part of the retina where the photoreceptor cells are freely accessible to the light coming in and where the ganglion cells do not overlap them. Only this tiny area of the retina ensures the maximum of visual acuity and image sharpness. The fovea centralis is the only part of the retina where **100 percent visual acuity** is possible. Here, the tiniest changes in image quality and in the position of the eyes are detected and that information is then immediately transmitted at maximum speed to the control areas of the brain's visual centers. That is why 80 percent of the fibers of the optic nerve originate from this tiny area of the retina and from there send information at high speed and at equal signal strength to **both brain hemispheres** at the same time in order to trigger adjustment and control reflexes.

Our brain detects almost instantaneously that the image sharpness needs to be adjusted when we look at the blackboard 20 feet away from us after looking only milliseconds before at the notebook within our near vision range 16 inches away from us. The axes of our eyes must simultaneously be adjusted to the new viewing distance of 20 feet, just moments after having accommodated a reading distance of only 16 inches. These efferent correcting reflexes sent from the brain to the eyes are always organized in **binocular** fashion and thus are always transmitted to both eyes at the same time and at equal signal strength.

3.10
THE PERFECT NETWORK: IMAGE FUSION

Because we have two eyes, our brain is always processing two images. Those images are centered on the same point with pinpoint accuracy thanks to the motor coordination of the eye muscles. Our brain then fuses the two images into one single image, a visual function called **fusion**. As a sensorimotor function of the brain, fusion perfectly connects the two components of perception (sensory function) and eye position (motor function). This process of perfect binocular alignment and coordination requires what is called **optimal fusional amplitude**. This term designates the perfectly fused binocular visual field for every conceivable viewing distance as well as the ability to immediately correct and fine-tune even the tiniest deviations in the eye's axis that can occur at each rapid gaze saccade. For example, when the eyes are positioned for near vision and one of the eyes slides inward, even if only by less than a hundredth of an inch, a fusion reflex corrects this deviation immediately and automatically.

The above-described sensorimotor reflexes can be measured as fusion amplitude that comprises in convergence (with both eye axes turned inward) about 20–40 prism units or diopters. When we are working in near vision range for longer periods of time – for example, when reading or writing – a sustained convergence effort is required. To relax the muscles, the corresponding opposite eye movement, namely, divergent fusion amplitude (nominal value of 10–20 prism diopters) is required. This alternation between convergence tension and release is always necessary. On the whole, the fusion of images is a very dynamic process of sensorimotor – fine-tuning that is efficiently organized through reflexes. Accurate and efficient fusional function is the foundation for good vision. We are usually unaware of the effort required from our eyes and brain to make this process run smoothly.

3.11
WHEN FUSION FAILS:
DOUBLE IMAGES OR SUPPRESSION

Let's return now to Laura's problems with copying text from the blackboard. As you may remember, her ability to control her eye muscles to produce convergence was severely limited. She suffered from convergence insufficiency (CI) and tried unconsciously to deal with this insufficiency by shifting her eyes towards the board where convergence was not required. She attempted to avoid frequent and rapid shifts between looking at the board and looking into her notebook to guide her hand movements as she was writing. Her fusion amplitude was practically nonexistent. Even tiny sideways glances, including a glance at the next word in the line, were enough to cause her fusion to fail.

READING WITH DOUBLE VISION

When fusion fails, there are only two ways for our brain to respond to images that do not match perfectly: we will either see two images in different places – that is, we will have double vision – or our brain temporarily switches off or suppresses the shifted image.

When fusion fails, there are only two ways for our brain to respond to images that are not perfectly aligned and so do not match perfectly. We will either see two images in different places – that is, we will have double vision – or our brain temporarily switches off or suppresses the image from one eye.

This temporary switching off of visual images is a perception disorder called **intermittent central suppression or ICS**. It involves temporary deletion or suppression of details of visual perception that can be brief. This disorder has nothing to do with the deep, long-lasting suppression of the perceptions of a squinting (or crossed) eye and the resulting visual deficiency called **amblyopia**. Neurophysiologically speaking, ICS is more like the temporary deletion of the image during very rapid gaze saccades, but in this disorder the suppression lasts much longer than in a saccade.

Intermittent central suppression is essentially a type of **functional disorder**. Often it **affects only lines or dots** and can cause a **rapid flickering of the image**. Obviously, this is an annoyance and makes recognizing the letters of the alphabet difficult. With this disorder our visual brain "protects" us from annoying double images, but also makes reading very strenuous.

3.12
3D: SEEING IN THE THIRD DIMENSION

Our ancestors used stereoscopic vision, known as the ability to see in three dimensions, to hunt for food or flee from enemies. They had to be able to assess how far away objects were and how they moved; and they had to do so quickly and accurately in order to respond appropriately. Nowadays, we need our stereoscopic vision to navigate safely in our much more dangerous and confusing environment like in traffic.

Stereoscopic vision is not an innate ability. We must learn it based on our experiences with the space around us and the objects in it. Our body's movements as well as our perceptions of touch and our sense of balance enable us to develop a three-dimensional map of our environment. We use our experience and numerous insights to develop an integrated understanding of the spatial aspects of our world.

For example, we have learned:

→   **My hand** is nearer to me than the horizon.

→   **Balls** are always uniformly round objects.

→   **Every box** has a front and a back side.

People who can see only with one eye also have the ability to draw accurate conclusions from insights into the characteristics of spatial dimensions. In fact, some people are so adept at this in terms of their motor skills that they can even play tennis or golf without having true stereoscopic vision.

Still, our physiological ability of 3D vision is based on being able to see with two eyes and thus always having two images with a slightly different perspective of objects we are looking at. Our right eye sees an object from the right side, the left eye slightly more from the left side. You can experience this effect for yourself by the following experiment. Hold your thumb up about 12 inches in front of your nose and alternately close first one eye and then the

We comprehend distances and spatial depth by means of:

→   **Perspective:** the farther away something is from us the smaller it will appear.

→   **Contour sharpness:** the farther away something is from us the less sharp its contours will appear.

→   **Shadows cast overlapping of objects:** An object is partially covered up by another? Then the object that is fully visible must be located in front of the one that's only partially visible.

---

other. You will see your thumb seemingly jumping back and forth from one side to the other even though it is not moving at all. The perception of movement is the result of seeing the thumb from a different perspective with each eye.

The vision centers in our brain process the two-dimensional images of the right and left eye optimally and "construct" a three-dimensional image from them, our stereoscopic or 3D vision. Thanks to this function we can assess distances at a glance, see how far away objects are from us and how fast they are moving. We can see the individual stairs of a staircase and know exactly at what depth we have to place our feet to safely go down the stairs. We recognize objects that move at great speeds, can assess the trajectory of tennis balls, and can react to them in an instant.

3D OR STEREOSCOPIC VISION

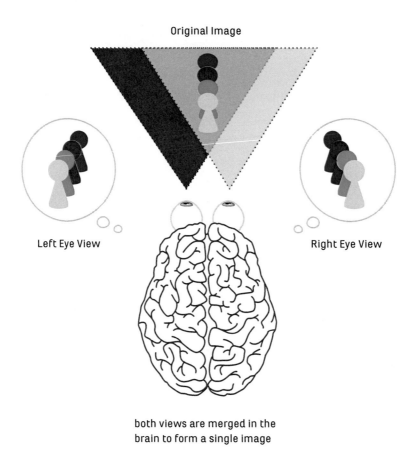

both views are merged in the
brain to form a single image

All ball sports require perfect 3D vision, and the accompanying motor coordination of the relevant muscles as well as the proper timing of all these processes, which have to run their course in a split second.

To ensure that this brain function works correctly even the smallest eye movements must be perfectly coordinated and fused.

3.13
PROBLEMS WITH SEEING IN THREE DIMENSIONS

For most people seeing a 3D film in the movie theater is great fun. However, about 10 percent of all children and adults feel very differently about this experience. Normally, our perception of three-dimensional depth is connected with the corresponding eye movements. When we are looking at something in near vision range, our eyes converge inward. When we are looking at something farther away, the axes of our eyes turn slightly outward. Watching a 3D film, however, calls for other skills, ones we do not usually use in our daily life.

When we are watching a 3D film, our **perceptual distance** to the screen remains **static**, and we keep our eyes fixed on it. Our brain, however, has to process two different images that are separated by color or polarization glasses. **For this we need a very stable fusional function.**

Many people who have insufficiencies or disorders of binocular vision but did not know they had them will have a surprisingly unpleasant experience when watching 3D movies. If they are among the 5 percent of people who have no stereoscopic vision at all, the movie will be a frustrating experience for them because they completely miss out on the enjoyment other people derive from such effects. Depending on the type and severity of their binocular vision disorder, some people suffer from headaches, dizziness, and nausea when they are watching a 3D movie.

School children with disorders of stereoscopic vision will feel the effect above all in sports; their performance suffers because they lack skill, speed, and accuracy. Often they do not like any kind of sports that require perfect visual functions.

Generally, these children's motor responses are comparatively slow and awkward. They cannot catch balls or correctly assess game situations that require a quick response. Because other players soon realize that these kids make it nearly impossible for the team to win, children with these visual disorders are often the last to be chosen for a ball sports team.

Perfect 3D vision and excellent visual performance are significant preconditions for nearly all types of sports.

This is not a matter of correctly reading the letters and symbols on the eye chart. For example, top athletes in tennis must have a high-speed dynamic visual acuity combined with flawless stereoscopic vision from any angle, no matter how oblique. And slalom racers must correctly assess the location, in relation to their own position, of obstacles they are approaching at very high speed – their life can depend on this ability.

Almost every mistake in sports is ultimately due to a visual error of judgement.

For example, in soccer or other team sports, players not only must exactly and correctly assess their own movements but also those of the ball and the dynamic movements of several other players they can see in their peripheral visual field. Likewise, in fencing or golf the players need similar, no less complicated visual abilities.

Dynamic seeing, contrast sensitivity, peripheral vision, assessment of the speed at which others move or of the trajectory of objects, reaction time, eye-hand-foot coordination, timing, split attention in the visual field and simultaneously optimal concentration on one's actions, are all visual skills qualified coaches know can be learned and improved with training.

That is why there are specialists for sports vision all over the world who develop training programs for top athletes to help them improve their visual performance in their sport.

ALMOST EVERY MISTAKE IN SPORTS IS ULTIMATELY DUE TO AN ERROR IN VISUAL JUDGEMENT.

HOW FAR AWAY IS IT?

110

100

90

80

70

60

50

40

30

20

10

4

Chapter

Diagnosing Disorders of Binocularity and Visual Perception

4

DIAGNOSING
DISORDERS OF BINOCULARITY AND VISUAL PERCEPTION

The symptoms observed in children with learning and concentration issues are often just the tip of the iceberg. They may suffer from several underlying and undetected visual dysfunctions. The more precisely typical symptoms are identified initially, the more effectively the diagnostic process can be targeted to the child's problems.

Looking at the notebooks, tests, and worksheets a child has worked on in the current school year can provide useful insights (see checklist at end of the chapter). Therefore, our diagnostic process begins with a thorough analysis of the child's daily schoolwork. To determine whether the child has a partial learning deficit or a part type of learning disorder, we administer not only the standard school performance tests – such as spelling, arithmetic, and reading tests – but also intelligence testing.

Our comprehensive visual assessment is based on a model of four interconnected circles that represent the fundamental functional components of vision, including the brain's complex visual information processing functions. This cybernetic model of synchronized and interdependent visual functions was created by the "father" of developmental optometry, the American optometrist Arthur Marten Skeffington to illustrate the complexity of vision.

While a detailed technical description of the diagnostic methodology would go beyond the scope of this book, for parents and teachers of children affected by disorders of visual functions and processing, this model enables us to understand the basic concepts of the diagnostic process.

CYBERNETIC MODEL OF PERFECT VISION

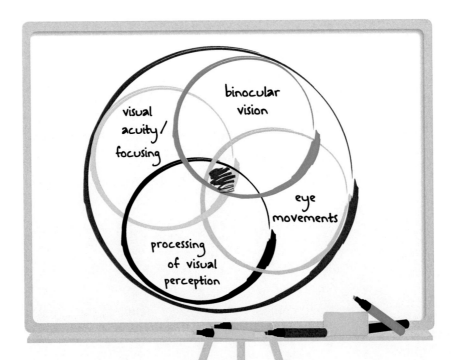

PARENTS ARE IMPORTANT PARTICIPATING OBSERVERS IN THE DIAGNOSTIC PROCESS

In our practice parents are present in the exam room during the entire process of diagnosing their child's visual problem, so they can see for themselves the components of our methods and what visual and processing functions are being tested. As they watch their child's reactions in some of the visual tests, parents can realize firsthand that even when all are looking at the same picture, their child's perception is very different from their own.

Parents experience daily the problems their child struggles with, and often they are even held responsible for the problems or or battle with feelings of guilt. Our approach allows parents to gain a deeper understanding of how visual perception works and offers them the opportunity to observe, ask questions about their child's visual functions and to discuss the diagnostic process and treatment in more detail.

Interestingly, this approach is also helpful for the children concerned, and they welcome it. We explain the examination as a joint research project to find out what difficulties the child is dealing with and what causes them. Even very young children can understand this approach and enter into the process in a spirit of exploration. Usually, by the time they come for Vision Therapy, the children and their families have already endured great emotional strain, frustration, and suffering because of their learning struggles and because they have already tried and failed many times at solving the problems. It's a great relief, then, for the parents and the child to see that testing is not about allocating blame or labeling anyone as incompetent or stupid. That's also why we invite the child's teachers if the child would like to have them present. Teachers are important and trusted persons in the child's life, and it is therefore especially helpful when teachers can see for themselves what their student's problem is.

→   **IN THE DIAGNOSTIC PROCESS WE ARE INTERESTED IN ALL COMPONENTS OF THE CYBERNETIC MODEL OF OPTIMAL VISUAL FUNCTION.**

4.01
VISUAL ACUITY

Testing monocular visual acuity is a fundamental step in any visual diagnostic process. If a child does not have perfect eyesight in each eye, the eye must be examined in more detail to rule out any disease and determine whether the child needs glasses. Tests must assess whether amblyopia is the reason for poorly developed acuity due to strabismus or major refractive errors. Other tests are needed to determine whether central foveolar fixation is possible. Children with visual acuity problems should also be examined for the relatively rare condition of microstrabismus with anomalous retinal correspondence, which leads to a particularly problematic form of binocular vision. Of course, before any therapy is started, all the above-mentioned conditions should be ruled out, and if the child needs glasses to correct hyperopia, myopia, or astigmatism, the appropriate corrective glasses should be prescribed.

In the context of visual perception and learning, monocular visual acuity is the only testing method that involves one eye at a time. It is most important to include acuity testing with both eyes. Our brain organizes and processes all visual functions in a binocular fashion. As already discussed, even children with 20/20 visual acuity in one eye at a distance of 20 feet can nevertheless suffer from significant binocular dysfunctions that affect even monocular perfect vision. For that reason we assess not only whether a child can read small numbers at a distance of 20 feet but also whether the child can see well with both eyes at near vision range of about 16 inches.

Flexible visual acuity, that is, the ability to see clearly at all distances, is not something to take for granted. That is why we also examine the dynamic aspects of vision like accommodative flexibility. This is the ability to perfectly adjust visual acuity to the viewing distance in just milliseconds. Thanks to this accommodative flexibility we can see clearly whether we are looking at our notebook, at the blackboard, or switching frequently between the two. Obviously, this function is absolutely essential for school children.

4.02
EYE MUSCLE FUNCTIONS

To assess the oculomotor functions of both eyes the following questions are clarified:

→ **Can the child** reliably and easily control his or her eyes so that steady fixation on a point is possible?

→ **Can the child** maintain steady fixation on a point even when asked to speak or do math calculations at the same time – that is, when the brain is busy with other tasks?

→ **Can the child** move his or her eyes in all viewing directions?

→ **Can the child** visually track a moving object with the eyes and do so smoothly, steadily, and precisely without needing corrective saccades?

→ **What does** this visual tracking look like horizontally, vertically, and sagitally?

→ **How well** can the child control movements of the eyes over a longer period of time?

→ **Can the child** perform smooth horizontal gaze saccades to scan a reading line of letters or symbols?

→ **Can the child** accurately move on to the next reading line or does his or her gaze sometimes land on a line below that?

→ **Are there** dysfunctions in the interaction of the 12 eye muscles?

———————————

As you have learned from the neurophysiology of vision (see chapter 3), testing eye muscle functions automatically involves testing the cranial nerves connected to them. The measurement of eye muscle coordination by coordimetry offers precise data to diagnose and quantify muscular dysfunctions. Functional tests, such as the Developmental Eye Movement Test (DEM), offer very detailed data on eye movements, tracking, and reading saccades. To assess reading performance we use infrared oculography.

4.03
BINOCULAR VISION

To assess the oculomotor functions of both eyes the following questions are clarified:

———————————

→ **How stable** and efficient are the child's binocular visual functions, the so-called binocular status?

→ **Does the child** have a convergence insufficiency (CI)?

→ **How stable** and resilient is the convergence?

→ **How stable** and resilient is the child's accommodation-convergence reflex?

→ **Does the child** show signs of latent strabismus with inward deviation (esophoria) or outward deviation (exophoria)?

→ **Are there** vertical axis deviations in certain viewing directions?

→ **Does the child** have double vision at a particular distance or in a particular direction of gaze?

→ **Does the child** show intermittent central suppression (ICS)?

→ **Does the child** have stable simultaneous visual perception?

→ **Does the child** have the ability to fuse the visual impressions from both eyes into one image?

→ **Does the child** have stable fusion amplitude at all viewing distances?

→ **Does the child** have optimal 3D vision at all distances?

4.04

BODY IMAGE, MOTOR SKILLS, PERSISTENT PRIMARY REFLEXES

→ **How does the child** perceive and move his or her own body? How well can he or she maintain equilibrium? Can the child maintain equilibrium and carry out visual tasks at the same time?

→ **How well** developed are the child's fine motor skills, graphomotor skills, and eye-hand coordination?

→ **Does the child** know where right and left is, on his or her own body and on others?

→ **How well** developed are the concepts of laterality and directionality?

→ **Does the child** have persistent primary reflexes?

If it is found that the child has persistent primary reflexes, our practice will recommend an appropriate therapy, and ideally that therapy should be completed before Vision Therapy begins. However, occupational therapists often prefer to wait for the completion of our Optometric Vision Therapy because their therapeutic success in treating visual perception processing and fine motor skills is considerably improved and speeded up when major visual neurophysiological dysfunctions have been eliminated first.

4.05
VISUAL PROCESSING DISORDER (VPD)

→   **Visual-motor coordination** – can eye movements be synchronized perfectly with movements of hands or body?

→   **Form constancy** – can the child recognize forms and objects as the same independent of their size, color, thickness, or the angle of view?

→   **Visual discrimination** – can the child see differences between objects that are similar?

→   **Visual figure-ground perception** – can the child distinguish shapes and objects from a visually structured background?

→   **Visual-spatial relationships and orientation** – can the child assess the position and spatial relationships of shapes and objects in relation to the child's own position in space? The relation of shapes and objects to an axis, to each other, and to the space around them?

→   **Visual Closure** – can the child visualize a whole when given incomplete information or a partial picture, that is, can the child complete the picture in the mind?

→   **Visual memory** – can the child recall the characteristics of a given object or form?

4.06

SIMULTANEOUS VISUAL PERCEPTION AND VISUAL SEQUENTIAL MEMORY

The next step in the diagnostic process covers abilities that are essential for reading, writing, and arithmetic. Specifically, we assess the child's ability in **simultaneous visual perception** – their ability to perceive at a glance the number of items seen. We also assess the child's visual memory for numbers, letters, and words in series.

→   **Can the child** perceive at one glance shapes and combinations of shapes including their details?

→   **Can** the child perceive at one glance a number combination, a letter combination, or an entire word?

→   **How many** items can the child perceive at one glance without error?

→   **At what speed** of presentation and perception can the child do this?

→   **Can the child** store the combination in short-term memory and recall it correctly?

→   **Can the child** do this successfully only verbally or also in writing?

→   **How fast**, how stable and error free does this phase of visual information processing operate?

We also test the child's ability to visualize, to develop mental images and to work with these images. For this purpose we use tasks requiring dynamic mental visual orientation in a virtual space or on a chess board that allows the child to position objects and to visualize movements in a two-dimensional structure. Another interesting task is the mental rotation of an abstract object. The child has to imagine a form, a letter, or a number, describe these in detail, and then rotate them as specified and instructed. For example, what would the letter "T" look like if you turned it upside down?

4.07
READING TECHNIQUE

It is always important to closely observe the reading technique of children struggling with difficulties. These kids usually do not like to read at all and in particular do not like reading aloud because that makes their slow reading and their mistakes apparent to others. Many children also automatically use their **index finger to support** their eyes' horizontal scanning movement along the line of text. Many also **move their head along** while reading. **Mistakes when moving from one line of text to the next** are also very common. For example, upon reaching the end of a line, instead of landing automatically at the beginning of the next line, their eyes may land on the line below or even skip two lines. Some children start reading at the **third letter of a word** or stop reading in the middle of a word and then continue reading with the word after the next. Their eyes do not automatically pause at the boundary of a word but randomly anywhere. Often these children **leave out entire words or word endings**.

Reading aloud is usually nearly as fast as speaking, and some children who need a lot of time to recognize a word and are painfully slow in reading then try to compensate by **guessing**. After all, guessing is much faster than their laborious reading and sounds better than slowly and painstakingly sounding out individual letters. Moreover, children with a knack for language can easily substitute a word based on just a few fragments. Their guesses may not be perfect but often make sense; for example, they may read "lawn" instead of "meadow" because they could identify an "a" and a "w." Still, for the most part this strategy does not work, and these kids often read aloud words that are not on the page and that do not fit into the context or meaning of the text read. As a result, their reading aloud makes no sense and leads to confusion and frustration.

Motor skills for reading

We examine complex tasks of the oculomotor system, such as controlling the eyes' horizontal movements for reading known as reading saccades very thoroughly with a variety of testing methods. Children who have already learned to read can be tested by means of highly differentiated so-called **infrared oculography**. In this test special measuring goggles use infrared cameras to register and record the movement patterns of the eyes during the reading process and then analyze these data in detail. The resulting measurements provide information about the speed at which a child reads. In addition, the **duration of gaze fixation** a child needs to recognize an individual word as well as the number of gaze fixations needed for a given number of words can be determined. Moreover, this test identifies **regressions** occurring during reading. Regressions are involuntary eye movements in the opposite direction of the normal reading flow. Regressions move from right to left. Obviously, they interfere with the smooth left to right movements of the eyes along the lines of text.

Thus, it is possible to assess with great precision how fast a child can read in terms of words per minute and also to gain information about **eye movement patterns, perceptual functions, and reading comprehension**.

4.08
AT A GLANCE: THE DIAGNOSTIC AND THERAPEUTIC PUZZLE OF VISUAL FUNCTIONS

Our **comprehensive diagnostic process** has developed based on neuro-physiological skills for visual efficiency and the variety and complexity of visual perception and information processing. More than **20 different areas in the brain** are involved in processing visual information. Essentially, through interconnection with other functions, about **80 percent of our brain** is actively involved in processing visual information. Visual perception enables us to quickly and precisely identify and respond to what we see during every motor activity, such as walking, driving, or playing tennis. Learning processes, such as learning to read and write, learning how to spell and how to correct spelling errors, learning new vocabulary and even to read or write in foreign languages, all have their roots in perfect visual skills.

When children develop learning difficulties, a thorough analysis of these brain functions is absolutely essential.

After testing and analyzing the individual visual functions in our diagnostic process, we use the picture of a jigsaw puzzle to show parents and child where the child's weaknesses and strengths are. This puzzle includes the most essential components of the diagnostic process and can easily be understood even by children. **In many cases, only a few of the components are missing or are weak in their functioning.**

However, these missing or fragile components can jeopardize the stability of the entire structure and compromise the child's learning success.

For example, a child affected by a combination of convergence insufficiency, accommodation problems, and fragile fusion with oculomotor deficits, confusion of the spatial position of letters such as b and d, and a slow rate of simultaneous perception for letter combinations will have significant learning difficulties.

Because of the hierarchical structure of our puzzle image, parents and children can easily understand the significance of basic functions and the interconnections between the various functional areas. Since practically all individual components of our diagnostic process deal with brain functions that are learned and developed, they can be taught and improved through Optometric Vision Therapy. The **Individual Training Plan** for therapy emerges logically from the puzzle picture our tests have yielded. With this in mind, we can also explain the different phases of the planned therapy program. This method allows children to see which component and which phase they are working on in their therapy.

It is a clear advantage, when children understand the reasons and goals for their work in Vision Therapy. Their participation is then based on insight and understanding of the relationships and interconnections between perception and learning. Their therapist will ask them frequently in the course of their therapy and also every time when new exercises are introduced: **"Can you explain to me how you will use in school what you are training now?"**

This so-called **Socratic method** encourages active and independent thinking and allows children to discover interconnections between functions for themselves. This approach works even with children of elementary school age. When kids no longer feel helpless and are no longer stuck in believing they can't succeed, they become active partners in their own therapy and sometimes even "invent" creative variations of individual exercises. On the whole our children in Vision Therapy are well aware that they are doing something for themselves, their own skills and success, and they understand why and how they are doing this.

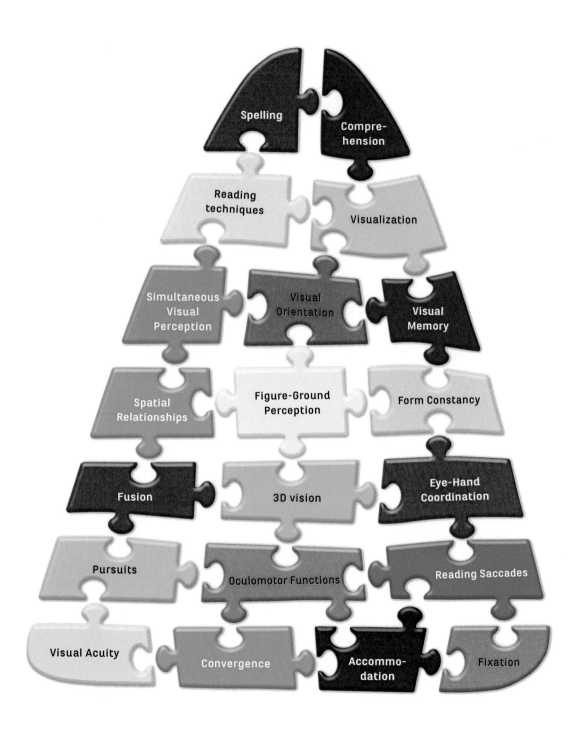

5
Chapter

A Complex Handicap:
Children with Combined Hearing
and Vision Problems

5

A COMPLEX
HANDICAP

Children with Combined
Hearing and Vision Problems

We have already explained in detail the learning problems
visual disorders can cause by themselves. But what happens
when additional problems of perception arise? Unfortunately some children begin their school years with a double
impairment their parents or teachers do not even know about.
Often, these kids attract attention because of their behavioral
problems that are, in fact, caused by an undetected hearing
impairment. Many affected children develop severe learning
and concentration problems. In this chapter, you will learn
about the difficulties preschoolers and school children can
experience when they suffer from problems with hearing
and auditory processing as well as from speech and language
problems.

5.01

WHAT DID YOU SAY?
DAVID´S EXPERIENCE IN KINDERGARTEN AND ELEMENTARY SCHOOL WITH UNDIAGNOSED HEARING AND SPEECH/LANGUAGE PROBLEMS

David was a content baby and a cheerful toddler when he was still at home with his parents. He was a bit slow in his speech development, and at the age of three years he could only say a few individual words, but no sentences. Still, he was able to express his wishes and needs well enough for his parents to understand him. They were worried because David often suffered from colds and inflammations of the middle ear (otitis media), but their pediatrician reassured them. The consulted otolaryngologist (ear, nose, and throat specialist) agreed and explained that children usually outgrow these illnesses and that at that early age many boys are a bit slower in speech development than girls. At the age of four, David started going to kindergarten. By that time he had already had 12 bouts of middle ear infection, some of them minor and some quite serious.

In kindergarten, he drew the teachers' attention right away because his ability to play with other children was not well developed. He clung to the teachers, could not communicate well with the other children, and quickly became aggressive when his usual strategy of pointing at things he wanted or simply taking them did not work. When he talked, the other children often could not understand him, and because of his unpredictable behavior they did not want to play with him. David was often sitting alone and unhappy in the corner with the building blocks. During the daily morning circle when the children took turns talking and sharing experiences and stories, David was very disruptive and did not participate in the conversation.

A few months later, during a routine checkup David's pediatrician found that the boy was slightly hard of hearing. The otolaryngologist David's parents consulted again now suggested an operation because David was also snoring very loudly. His nasal polyps were so enlarged that they narrowed his airways. Thus, at the age of five, David had surgery during which a ventilation tube (also known as tympanostomy tube or T-tube) was implanted into each eardrum. During the operation, the doctors found that David was suffering from a chronic seromucinous otitis. This means that David's middle ear, which houses the ossicular chain, was filled with thick, viscous mucus that had to be suctioned off. The vent tubes were implanted to ensure consistent ventilation of the middle ear so it would be well supplied with air even when David had a cold or the sniffles.

In the hearing test following the operation David did much better, and the pediatrician now prescribed logotherapy (speech and language therapy). The diagnosis on the prescription was **delayed speech development with multiple dyslalia** (a disorder in pronunciation and articulation of several speech sounds) as well as **dysgrammatism**, a problem with consistently forming grammatically correct sentences. For example, David sometimes said:

"I GOED HOME NOW,"

or asked other children for toys by saying:

"I THIS WANT, YOU NOW
ME GIVE THIS!"

Thanks to the friendly and competent therapist, David's speech and language therapy went well. David enjoyed the therapy sessions, participated well, and made rapid progress in his speech development. He was soon able to speak more clearly and his vocabulary grew day by day. In kindergarten, he was now a completely well adjusted child, who could peacefully communicate and play with the other children.

The speech therapy was continued until shortly before David was enrolled in elementary school, when it was considered successfully concluded. When

David was examined before starting first grade, no cause for concern was found.

However, closely listening to David revealed several minor "irregularities" in his speech. For example, sometimes he mispronounced words, saying **"polomotive"** instead of **"locomotive."** He seemed not to be able to pronounce object case endings. For example he did not differentiate between **"he"** and **"him,"** and the sounds **"n"** and **"m"** were identical to him. His sentences were generally still very short and not always grammatically correct. For instance, David still said,

"I WENTED INTO THE WOODS"

or

"I CHOCOLATE WANT."

However, his speech therapist said David had the ability to pronounce everything correctly but just had to make more of an effort.

At the same time, David showed extreme sensitivity to noise. He hated going to the indoor swimming pool and the gym because of the many loud children there. During the morning circle in kindergarten he still had difficulty listening to other children and contributing to the conversation himself.

David's mother noticed that he could not retell even very short stories correctly. When he was trying to tell his parents about something, they often had to remind him to slow down and talk about one thing at a time. His stories often lacked a unifying common thread or theme, and it was often difficult to understand who had done what and when.

David's kindergarten teachers reported that he often did not do what was asked of him. At home also there were often conflicts because when instructions were a bit complicated, David did not follow them. For example, if he was asked to:

"GO INTO THE KITCHEN AND TAKE THE BROOM THAT'S UNDER THE SINK ON THE LEFT. PLEASE BRING IT OUT TO ME IN THE GARDEN."

After such instructions, the parents would find David standing in the kitchen, clearly at a loss about what he was supposed to do or fetch. Often David left the room without doing what he was told, and his parents were frustrated with his lack of helpfulness and his behavioral problems. When David's parents had friends over and were sitting around the table talking with several people, David would ask questions that showed that he had not been able to follow the conversation. He often withdrew from such situations, left the table, and went off to play by himself.

David began to have problems in school in the first few months of first grade. He often took a long time to do his assignments, did not comprehend what he was supposed to do, and imitated or copied from the child next to him. The teacher became increasingly frustrated because she always had to tell David everything more than once, and he was very slow in learning to read and write. When David had to write words, it was often hard to recognize what words he had written; his writing was illegible.

The teacher expected that learning to write based on the phonetic spelling method would help the children to enjoy writing and have fun writing stories. But in David's case, this expectation fell short. He did not learn to spell phonetically and was unable to say words aloud to himself and then write them down based on what he had heard himself say. In first grade, the teacher would have seen

"MONSTA" AND "RITIN"

as acceptable ways of writing the words "monster" and "writing." However, David wrote:

"MNT" AND "RINT."

He could not reliably and consistently identify the initial or last letters of words and very quickly lost all interest in writing.

When he was reading, David had trouble recognizing the words he had just laboriously spelled out even if they consisted of only three letters. As a result, he did not understand at all what stories were about and soon began to hate reading. Strangely enough, in kindergarten he had also not enjoyed listening when stories were read aloud, and he always quickly withdrew when his mother wanted to read stories to him. Thus, she was unsurprised that her boy developed reading problems. Soon, homework became a painful ordeal for David and his mother. Usually, his mother had to start by calling other parents to find out what the homework assignment was because David rarely knew what he was supposed to do. His mother tried to explain to him what he had to do, but that did not help either. Since David could not write any words by himself, she finally decided to dictate his homework to him and to write things for him because otherwise his notebook would have remained empty.

Her talks with David's teacher were depressing. The teacher was frustrated because of his poor concentration and his inability to listen closely and follow assignment instructions. The teacher usually had to remind him several times. She was also frustrated by his lack of motivation and his copying from other children. The teacher mentioned the term "learning disability" and suggested that David should be observed and tested by a school psychologist. By the end of first grade, David still could not do any of the things the other children had long since learned. The school psychologist explained that advancing to second grade was out of the question for David.

David's parents were greatly worried, and up to then there had been no indication in their family's daily life that David might perhaps not have normal intelligence. They were concerned that David might have to be in special education classes and might already now, at the end of first grade, be on a path that would make graduating normally with a diploma impossible for him.

The specialists the parents consulted – the pediatrician, the pediatric otolaryngologist, and the speech therapist – had assured them that David's hearing and speech and language problems had been treated successfully before he started school. Neither the parents nor the teachers suspected that David's learning difficulties were caused by auditory and speech processing problems that still persisted. David was suffering from an undiagnosed auditory processing disorder also called Central Auditory Processing Disorder (CAPD).

5.02
HOW A CENTRAL AUDITORY PROCESSING DISORDER (CAPD) DEVELOPS

The preceding chapters explained in detail how complicated the various aspects of visual perception and processing are. Much the same applies also to hearing and speech processing.

The hearing tests conducted as part of routine checkups with a pediatrician or otolaryngologist are concerned only with the so-called audiometry. Like the ophthalmologist's visual acuity tests, these hearing tests are the basic first step in testing children's hearing and are thus an indispensable tool for the diagnosis of hearing difficulties from any cause. These tests work with a stimulus that is not part of our normal world of hearing. That is, artificially created sinusoidal tones are used to determine the patient's hearing threshold. The hearing threshold is defined as the very lowest loudness level at which an individual tone is just barely audible.

Disorders related to the hearing threshold cause hearing difficulty or hearing loss. The latter can take two forms: in rare cases children can suffer from **sensorineural or inner ear hearing loss** caused by congenital or acquired damage to the auditory nerve. In contrast, **conductive hearing loss** is much more common in children. Conductive hearing loss occurs when sound is not conducted efficiently through the outer ear canal to the eardrum and the tiny bones (ossicles) of the middle ear. As a result, the ability to hear faint sounds and a range of sound levels is reduced. In most cases this type of hearing loss is caused by middle ear infections (otitis media). During such infections the Eustachian tube swells up and thus impedes the ventilation of the middle ear. In many children this effect can be caused even by just a cold. Then the membranes swell, and bacterial colonization of the middle ear can cause fluid discharge and ultimately leads to **otitis media with effusion**. Fluid collects behind the child's eardrum, which can lead to severe ear aches, and makes the child, to a greater or lesser extent, hard of hearing. Since the ossicular chain that transmits sound is located in the tympanic cavity, and the chain can no longer properly vibrate and accurately conduct sound, this condition is called conductive hearing loss.

A particularly serious type of middle ear infection is not accompanied by fever or much pain. As it is almost entirely without symptoms, it is often undetected and untreated, and can persist for a longer period of time. Even just a relatively minor cold and the sniffles can lead to a chronic middle ear infection. In children such infections can cause impaired hearing that lasts for several weeks. It is possible nobody else notices the impairment, but it can have dire consequences because every middle ear infection leads to a more or less pronounced conductive hearing loss.

If such prolonged impairments of hearing occur during the critical phases of speech development, between the first and sixth year of life, their consequences are much worse than minor hearing loss that disappears completely after a few days or weeks. Instead, the child's more complex auditory processing and speech development can be impaired. Even when children's audiometric tests are normal, and they can hear very soft individual tones and sounds, an auditory processing disorder can make it very difficult or impossible for them to properly process heard information that consists of several components. In particular, processing and understanding speech and language information in daily life can become extremely difficult for children with such impairments.

5.03
SYMPTOMS OF A CENTRAL AUDITORY PROCESSING DISORDER (CAPD)

Auditory processing disorders affect the child's ability to listen, comprehend, and respond to spoken information. This can include problems with: sound localization and lateralization, binaural fusion, auditory discrimination, auditory pattern recognition, temporal aspects of audition, including temporal integration, temporal discrimination, temporal ordering, as well as auditory performance with competing acoustic signals including dichotic listening.

Among the symptoms of such disorders are problems with **discriminating between speech and background noises**, which is the auditory equivalent to visual figure-ground perception. The ability to understand details of speech even in the presence of background noises can be severely limited in children with such a disorder. The serious consequences in the child's daily life are obvious, as many kindergarten and school classrooms are filled with background noises.

Phonological awareness is the ability to analyze speech sounds one hears in order to learn how to spell a word correctly. It can also be seriously impaired. Another typical symptom of central auditory processing disorder affects the **auditory working memory**. The enormous significance of the auditory working memory for learning to read and write was described in detail in chapter 1. Likewise, children's auditory storage capacity, that is the ability to recall task instructions, the sequence of letters to read or write words, series of sentences, to deal with complex texts in which several characters are doing different things, can be severely limited. In that case, the affected children cannot learn to read, write, or properly follow a story they are reading or hearing, and consequently quickly lose any interest and enjoyment in listening.

Similar to the process of seeing with both eyes, auditory processing is based on sensory information from two sources, namely the auditory perceptions of the two ears. What happens in that process is very similar to what happens in our brain with the fusion of the two images from our eyes into one image. Thus, if during a middle ear infection one ear provides information of very poor quality, the perceptual processing connected to both ears is impaired.

In that case, the affected children can develop difficulties with **dichotic hearing**, the ability to hear and understand simultaneous, competing speech information. Clearly, this is an important function of our hearing in daily life. A child with functioning dichotic hearing can listen to the teacher explaining important information while at the same time responding to another child asking for an eraser.

In such situations children who lack the ability of dichotic hearing either hear the teacher or the other child but cannot process both impressions at the same time. They are **not** easily distracted or inattentive; rather, an auditory processing disorder prevents them from correctly perceiving different items of speech information that are present at the same time. Of course, situations with competing simultaneous speech perceptions are very common in kindergarten and school classrooms, and this adds to the difficulties the affected child must struggle with every day.

A disorder like deficient dichotic hearing makes it very difficult and exhausting for the child to understand everything being said in a conversation involving several people. Whenever possible, children suffering from auditory processing disorder avoid such stressful situations or quickly withdraw from them. This behaviour proves ineffective in academic settings. Moreover, due to disorders affecting their auditory working memory, these kids often are not sure what their teacher told them to do. Of course, they find it difficult to follow instructions and do assignments they cannot remember completely or accurately.

Naturally, children want to avoid the embarrassment of having to ask for instructions to be repeated and definitely want to avoid being scolded for not paying attention. They often resort to orienting himself by observing and following the example of the other children around them. Just as naturally, teachers and the affected children's classmates usually interpret this behavior as "copying" and consider it inappropriate or wrong.

Do you remember David's situation described above? If you reread that description of his struggles in kindergarten and school while keeping in mind what you now know about auditory processing disorders, you will better understand his problems with communication, listening, understanding, responding, and learning. These difficulties were caused by an undiagnosed auditory perceptual disorder.

CHILDREN WITH CAPD DO NOT UNDERSTAND WHAT PEOPLE IN A GROUP CONVERSATION ARE TALKING ABOUT AND TRY TO AVOID SUCH SITUATIONS OR QUICKLY WITHDRAW.

5.04
RECOGNIZING AUDITORY PROCESSING DISORDERS

The following checklist captures the typical symptoms of auditory processing disorders. If you have to place a checkmark next to more than two items for your child, a thorough examination by a specialized pediatric otolaryngologist is highly recommended.

CHECKLIST

AUDITORY PROCESSING DISORDERS AFFECT THE CHILD'S ABILITY TO LISTEN, COMPREHEND, AND RESPOND TO SPOKEN INFORMATION.

- Reacts poorly in loud or echoing rooms
- Noticeable noise sensitivity
- Asks questions for reassurance, problems in following directions
- Much better understanding of tasks and assignments in one-on-one situations
- Finds it difficult to participate in group conversations
- Often looks to see what others are doing
- Pronunciation errors persist a long time
- Confuses words that sound alike: them/then, fish/dish, head/bed
- Answers that are not related to the content of the question
- Actions do not correspond to the content of the task instructions
- Only brief and slight interest in stories or none at all
- Poor auditory memory, both in duration and sequence (unable to recount sentences, stories, or task instructions or to spell out longer words)

5.05
DIAGNOSIS OF AUDITORY PROCESSING DISORDERS

Disorders of auditory processing can develop as a consequence of a long-standing hearing defect and often appear in combination with a developmental delay in language acquisition. In rare cases, such disorders also appear on their own without any other impairment of hearing or speech. The diagnostic process for disorders of auditory perception and processing is extensive and complex. It includes several specialized hearing tests as well as a thorough assessment by a speech and language pathologist. For preschoolers, the diagnostic process can be conducted by a certified **pediatric audiologist** or in the pediatric department of a university medical center's otolaryngology clinic.

Children diagnosed with a disorder of auditory processing are entitled to a corresponding therapy, which is carried out by specialized speech and language therapists. Moreover, in school these children are in need of special accommodations in the classroom and the aid and support of a specially trained speech and language teacher. Appropriate therapy often has to be continued over the long term, but considerable improvements in perceptual and processing functions are achievable in almost all cases.

5.06
CHILDREN WITH HEARING IMPAIRMENTS RELY ON A HEIGHTENED SENSE OF VISION

By now it should be clear that undiagnosed visual perceptual disorders can cause serious difficulties for children in school. When these children then also suffer from an undetected auditory processing problem, they are practically programmed for failure in school. Comprehensive testing of all relevant visual and auditory functions is absolutely essential for all school children with learning problems. Even when an auditory processing disorder has already been identified and treated before the child starts first grade, it is still extremely important to test these children's visual functions and also their ability to compensate visually for their deficits in hearing and understanding. **All children with auditory processing disorders and delayed speech and language development need an especially thorough and comprehensive assessment of their visual functions by a developmental optometrist.** The therapy of a speech development disorder and/or a processing disorder can take a very long time and last until the later years of elementary school. Visual compensation for hearing impairments is key to keep the affected children from failing in school.

Countless learning processes involving reading, writing, spelling, and math are controlled visually and are decisive for successful learning in school. In our experience, school children with a combination of visual and auditory perceptual disorders can benefit greatly from Optometric Vision Therapy. With improved visual functions, which can often be achieved within one year, these children will be able to better compensate for their auditory deficits.

COMPREHENSIVE TESTING OF ALL RELEVANT VISUAL AND AUDITORY FUNCTIONS IS ESSENTIAL FOR ALL SCHOOL CHILDREN WITH LEARNING PROBLEMS.

6

Chapter

What Parents
Can Do

6

WHAT PARENTS
CAN DO

Now that you have learned about how undetected disorders of visual functions and processing can affect your child's ability to learn, concentrate, and succeed in school, the following checklists will help you assess your child's situation in more detail and with greater certainty. Although the checklists have specific headings, there can be considerable overlap in signs and symptoms since many of these disorders affect more than one area of visual performance. Moreover, different disorders can cause symptoms that are very similar or the same.

6.01
CHECKLISTS FOR ASSESSING VISUAL PERCEPTION DISORDERS

PRACTICE DR. SCHUHMACHER

CHECKLIST –
EYESIGHT AND FOCUSING

FREQUENCY?	Never 0	Rarely 1	Sometimes 2	Often 3	Always 4
Blinks/squints, rubs his/her eyes, frowns, when copying writing?	○	○	○	○	○
Keeps a conspicuously short distance from notebook or reading material?	○	○	○	○	○
Shows strong aversion to writing tasks?	○	○	○	○	○
Complains of blurred vision when looking up from notebook to blackboard?	○	○	○	○	○
Has poor handwriting that keeps getting worse?	○	○	○	○	○
Separates words with spaces that vary in size?	○	○	○	○	○
Makes more mistakes toward the end of writing tasks?	○	○	○	○	○
Becomes fatigued very quickly and takes "unmotivated" breaks?	○	○	○	○	○
Has a short concentration span?	○	○	○	○	○
Complains of headaches and stomach-aches during reading and writing tasks?	○	○	○	○	○

PRACTICE DR. SCHUHMACHER

CHECKLIST -
EYE MOVEMENTS

FREQUENCY?	Never 0	Rarely 1	Sometimes 2	Often 3	Always 4
Shows aversion to reading and comes up with endless excuses to avoid reading?	○	○	○	○	○
Often guesses when reading or reads words that are not on the page?	○	○	○	○	○
Becomes disoriented in reading when moving from one line to the next?	○	○	○	○	○
Leaves out words in reading, omits letters or beginning or ending of words?	○	○	○	○	○
Clearly moves his or her head to follow along when reading?	○	○	○	○	○
Reads better when tracing the lines with a finger?	○	○	○	○	○
Reads very slowly but still does not understand written assignments?	○	○	○	○	○
Has considerable problems working with number lines, graph paper, tables, and charts?	○	○	○	○	○

PRACTICE DR. SCHUHMACHER

CHECKLIST -
BINOCULAR VISION

FREQUENCY?	Never 0	Rarely 1	Sometimes 2	Often 3	Always 4
Complains of double vision when reading?	◯	◯	◯	◯	◯
Closes one eye when working or covers one eye with a hand?	◯	◯	◯	◯	◯
Turns his or her head away, to work with one eye when reading or writing?	◯	◯	◯	◯	◯
Writes with margins that are conspicuously crooked or slanted?	◯	◯	◯	◯	◯
Has words and numbers "sliding" off the lines when writing on lined or quadrille ruled paper?	◯	◯	◯	◯	◯
Complains of letters "sliding" or "jumping around" – of "wobbling" lines in the notebook or squares on quadrille ruled paper?	◯	◯	◯	◯	◯

PRACTICE DR. SCHUHMACHER

CHECKLIST – VISUAL PROCESSING

FREQUENCY?	Never 0	Rarely 1	Sometimes 2	Often 3	Always 4
Confuses, reverses, or transposes letters or syllables, for example: p/q, b/d, ie/ei, da/ab, etc.?	◯	◯	◯	◯	◯
Does not recognize a word he or she has read just a few lines earlier?	◯	◯	◯	◯	◯
Spells words phonetically because of problems visualizing them	◯	◯	◯	◯	◯
Spells the same word in various phonetically correct but orthographically wrong ways when writing from dictation?	◯	◯	◯	◯	◯
Fails at comprehending and processing geometric tasks (such as axes errors, wrong proportions, wrong assignment of points?	◯	◯	◯	◯	◯

Analysis

If your child's **score adds up to more than 30 points**, it is fairly safe to assume that the factor **"undetected visual function and processing disorder"** plays a role in your child's learning difficulties.

If you have already consulted a pediatric ophthalmologist, his first step will have been to rule out significant physiological vision problems, such as retinopathy of prematurity, congenital defects, diabetic retinopathy, and cancers such as retinoblastoma. In addition, your child will have been examined for functional problems, such as strabismus or amblyopia. If you already know that your child's visual acuity is impaired by refractive disorders, such as nearsightedness, farsightedness, or astigmatism, have your child wear the prescribed glasses and then see whether your child's problems with reading and writing will disappear as a result of wearing the glasses.

If the prescribed glasses have little or no effect on your child's school work, or if the eye doctor found no impairment in the organic functions of your child and certified that your child has "eyes like a hawk" and 20/20 visual acuity in both eyes, then it is time to pursue additional tests and exams.

→   **You should consult a specialized developmental optometrist to have your child's learning-related visual functions assessed.**

6.02
WHERE TO FIND HELP FOR YOUR CHILD: DIAGNOSIS AND TREATMENT

If you have already consulted with a pediatric ophthalmologist, you might have found he was assisted by an orthoptist who evaluated your child's visual functions. The name of this medical specialty "orthoptics" is derived from the Greek term "orthos" meaning "straight" or "right" and "optic" meaning "sight." Orthoptics was fairly widely practiced in Germany decades ago, with orthoptists focusing on actively treating strabismus and disorders of binocular vision. Patients could consult a pediatric ophthalmologist's practice for active vision training, as they do with speech and language therapists or occupational therapists.

Unfortunately, active orthoptic training to improve visual functions has largely gone out of fashion and fallen into disuse. Instead, the standard treatment is now to prescribe the best possible glasses and in the case of amblyopia to cover the better-seeing eye with a patch. Strabismus surgery became the standard practice among pediatric ophthalmologists to correct muscle problems that cause deviations in the alignment of the eyes. When the "cosmetic" result of the operation is not satisfactory, often more operations follow.

In contrast, the science of active Vision Therapy – drug-free and nonsurgical – has flourished for many decades in the English-speaking areas of the world. In part, this is a result of the long-standing fact that in those countries the eye care field is served by two academic professions, namely, by ophthalmologists, trained in medical school, and by optometrists, trained in a college of optometry and also graduating with a doctoral degree. Training in developmental optometry focuses on the functional aspects of vision and the associated cerebral areas of visual processing. In contrast, pediatric ophthalmologist tend to look at the eye in isolation, without clinical involvement in the communication between the eyes and the rest of our brain and body. Developmental optometry is concerned with disorders of visual functions and their influence on the overall development of children's motor, sensory, and cognitive capacities. Decades of diagnostic insights have led to the development of a large and very active field of Optometric Vision Therapy offering drug-free and nonsurgical treatment options for children and adults. These therapy procedures are readily available in most English-speaking and many European countries.

In the United States you can contact and get information about certified developmental optometrists from the **College of Optometrists in Vision Development (COVD, www.covd.org)**, the largest professional association for optometrists that is active both nationally and internationally. It offers continuing scientifically based education and training for optometrists, coordination of research projects, and certification for specialized developmental optometrists and vision therapists.

→ **OEPF,** Optometric Extension Program Foundation (www.oepf.org)

→ **BOAF,** Behavioral Optometry Academy Foundation BOAF (www.boaf-eu.org)

→ **BABO,** British Association of Behavioral Optometrists (www.babo.co.uk)

Another important international organization is **the Optometric Extension Program Foundation (OEPF, www.oepf.org)**, which is dedicated to the advancement of the discipline of optometry through the gathering and dissemination of information on vision and the visual process. OEPF educates optometrists and their staff regarding the concepts of clinical vision care and makes a directory of clinical associates available on request.

In Germany, you will find a list of qualified and certified behavioral optometrists working in Austria, Germany, and Switzerland on the website of the Scientific Association for Ophthalmic Optics and Optometry **(Wissenschaftliche Vereinigung für Augenoptik und Optometrie, WVAO, www.wvao.org).** In other European countries, you can find lists of certified behavioral optometrists on the websites of various organizations, such as the **Behavioral Optometry Academy Foundation (BOAF, www.boaf-eu.org)** and the **British Association of Behavioral Optometrists (BABO, www.babo.co.uk)**.

6.03
WHAT YOUR CHILD'S TEACHERS NEED TO KNOW

If your child is diagnosed with a disorder of visual function and processing, it is essential to let your child's teachers know. Teachers usually assume that the children in their classes can see and hear well. It is rare for teachers to know anything about visual and auditory perceptual disorders, as these are only identified by specialized examinations and not with standard screening tests. It is therefore especially important for educators to have specific information from experts and therapists on how to help children affected by perceptual and processing disorders.

In general, school children's basic eyesight and hearing functions are not typically checked regularly as part of the care they receive in schools. In contrast, in Japan this subject is taken very seriously, and all children undergo regular eye and hearing screening tests twice a year from before they start school to graduation. These tests have been designed so they can be administered by teachers and school nurses. If significant changes in a child's perceptual functions are found, a professional assessment by a physician is the next step.

6.04
SUPPORTING MEASURES AND ACCOMMODATIONS AVAILABLE FOR CHILDREN WITH VISUAL DISABILITIES

If your child has been diagnosed with a visual function and processing disorder, you probably wonder how this will affect your child's schooling. For such cases the school system in every state provides for so-called **accommodations, supporting measures or specific assistance designed to help students with functional disorders** meet the requirements for school achievement and to compensate for difficulties or impairments in learning or performance.

Generally, to arrange for accommodations to help your child's learning in school, you need to request an evaluation from the school or school district. Upon completion of additional testing and evaluation, a team that includes at least one parent and the professionals working with your child will develop a plan calles an **Individualized Education Program (IEP)** that outlines the goals or progress to be achieved each year and details the specific services and accommodations to be provided in school to enable your child to achieve the goals agreed on.

For example, in Germany, you and your child's school can consult a specialized teacher for the blind and visually impaired. Since 2012 these educators are entrusted to provide help for children in regular classrooms. In addition to working with students who have physical visual impairments, low vision, or multiple disabilities, these specialized teachers also help kids suffering from the above-described visual functional and processing disorders. Of course, such teachers are not therapists and thus do not offer treatment, but they can advise your child's teachers regarding supportive measures that are possible and reasonable to implement in the classroom.

In general, to fulfill their educational mandate for all children, schools must provide reasonable accommodations for children diagnosed with functional disorders. Among the accommodations your child may be offered are appropriate changes to the design of teaching and classroom materials. These may be special lighting and slanted desks, permission to use technical devices, such as tablets with reading out loud functions and a camera so the child does not need to copy from the blackboard, enlarged worksheets and books, textbooks available in pdf format so students can enlarge the display as needed, and being allowed additional time to complete particular tasks or assignments.

Additional time is especially important for children with visual processing disorders because their very slow reading speed puts them at a great disadvantage in classroom work and tests. These children take a long time to read their assignments and instructions. As a result by the time they comprehend these often complex texts, they have little time left for completing the assigned task before time is up. Accordingly, one of the accommodations for children who cannot read assignments in the allotted time by themselves can be for the teacher to read the assignment or instructions aloud. Even children who can read these texts by themselves often take three times as long as their peers before they understand the instructions and can begin work on the assignment. To compensate for this difficulty, the affected children can be given correspondingly more time to complete an assignment.

In the United States the **No Child Left Behind Act (NCLB)**, a 2002 update of the Elementary and Secondary Education Act (ESEA) that made full educational opportunity a national priority, established a greater federal role in holding schools accountable for student outcomes. These laws set high standards in various fields, and your child might have to take assessments required under NCLB. Students with disabilities are allowed special accommodations when taking these state assessments. Special accommodations must be determined by the student's IEP team or Section 504 team, teams that usually also include you as the student's parent. The accommodations should be based on the student's **individual needs** and should be similar to those provided to the student during classroom assessments. Decisions about assessment accommodations are to be made on the basis of the student's needs, not on the basis of his or her disability category. Therefore, schools should not develop a standard list of accommodations to be automatically provided for all students with learning disabilities. Under NCLB, accommodations are defined as changes in testing materials or procedures that ensure that an assessment measures the student's knowledge rather than the student's disability.

A developmental optometrist experienced in dealing with children who have learning disabilities or impairments is well-equipped to document the visual problems that warrant classroom or testing modifications and accommodations.

If the above-described disorders of visual functions and processing continue to affect your child's learning in high school, you can ask for similar accommodations to be provided when your child takes the **American College Test (ACT) or the Scholastic Aptitude Test (SAT)** standardized tests to determine whether a high school graduate is prepared to do college-level work. If your child's disability is diagnosed and documented by a credentialed professional and the disability directly impacts performance SAT's or ACT's assessments, your child is entitled to a range of accommodations, from extended time for taking the test to what is called Special Testing. While the basic extended time accommodation allows students to take up to 50 percent more time than otherwise allocated, students eligible for Special Testing are allowed up to 100 percent additional time for completing the test. In addition, if your child is eligible for Special Testing, which is administered by the school's testing coordinator (TC), other reasonable accommodations can be provided, such as a private testing room, taking the test over several days, alternative test formats, and the presence of a support animal. The accommodations allowed depend on the nature and extent of the student's disability. For instance, a student with a visual processing disorder that severely limits reading speed may be permitted to take the ACT in four sittings over four days with double time allowed for completion of the test.

Lighting, Sitting Position, and Working Materials in School

The developmental optometrist providing therapy for your child or the educator for the blind and visually impaired consulting with your child's school can give you detailed information on the font sizes that are easier to read for your child and will perhaps suggest that all your child's printed work materials should be enlarged.

For example, worksheets and in-class assignments are often printed in an 8-point typeface and copied on grayish recycled paper, with copied text looking slightly blurry, not crisp and clear. If the worksheets are covered with many drawings and offer only little space for writing, they present a special challenge for children with visual difficulties. This problem of too much visual information on the page is called "crowding." Crowding can impair your child's ability to scan and identify visual items on the page even when visual acuity is normal. Very young children in particular are greatly affected by crowding, and for children with developmental delays crowding can cause difficulties for many years.

When crowding is eliminated, teachers are often surprised at how much the affected children's learning abilities and performance improve just because the working materials are enlarged so that no more than two tasks are on a white sheet of letter-size paper. Sometimes children even have twice as many correct answers as without the accommodation. **Clearly, enlarged and well-structured worksheets are a great help for all children and particularly important for those struggling with perceptual disorders.**

In addition, developmental optometrists can also advise you on the optimal lighting conditions for your child's desk or work area in the classroom and where in the classroom your child should be sitting. Specifically, children with visual function and processing problems should always sit so that they face the board straight on. When they have to copy anything from the board, the change in sight distance from their notebook or other writing surface to the board and back again is already a challenge for these children, and as a result many suffer from chronic headaches. Some children are so slow in visual comprehension that they should temporarily be spared such copying tasks. Otherwise they will still sit at their desk busy with writing during recess or will have to complete their work at home in addition to their daily homework assignments. It will be a great help to provide these children with large-print copies of the texts that they can start working on right away or, as mentioned before, to get technical help from a tablet computer.

You can easily confirm whether such copying tasks pose an excessive challenge to your child, even if your child does not bring home unfinished tasks from school. Many children facing homework assignments that require copying a text beg and urge their parents to dictate the text to them because for these kids copying is an extremely challenging task. As they struggle with visual disorders, these children often make more mistakes in copying text than when writing from dictation. Since they must correct those mistakes after copying, which is a time-consuming process, these kids have double the usual workload.

Looking at the Board: Never on a Slant

The cluster arrangement of desks that lets students sit in small groups and is common in many classrooms inevitably results in some students sitting sideways or even with their back to the board. A "skewed" or **slanted line of sight** to the board presents a significant challenge to strained eye muscles; therefore, such seating **should be avoided at all costs**.

In addition, having to turn the head to see the board can lead to long-term tension and tightness in the neck muscles and can cause damage to the cervical spine. In fact, constantly moving and turning the head while reading and writing is a great effort for all children, making it difficult for them to concentrate, conditions unacceptable for children with any visual problem.

Computer work stations in schools are also sometimes ill-advised and **not well-designed**. Children often have to work at desks and monitors that are placed too high. As a result, the kids always have to look up at the monitor. Getting our eyes to converge while looking upward places unnatural demands on the eye muscles and causes considerable visual fatigue. Of course, this is true especially for children, and all the more so for kids who are already dealing with visual problems.

6.05
HOW TO DESIGN AN OPTIMAL WORKSPACE FOR YOUR CHILD

The design and look of the workspace is particularly important for children dealing with visual difficulties. Begin by looking closely at the workspace together with your child. If there are many items on the desk, remove all those that are not essential. Any items drawing visual attention make visual concentration more difficult for your child and are distracting. What has proven most helpful is to have the desk clear of everything except the materials for the task being worked on at the moment. It is best to move the items that usually accumulate on and around your child's workspace away so they are entirely out of sight.

→ **Create an empty restful place for the eyes to work**

Make sure that the room has good ambient lighting and use a glare-free desk lamp placed so it casts light from your child's left side. To see and work at near distances requires a slight inclination of the head, which supports the convergence position of the eye axes. To allow a vertical view onto the writing and reading material, the **desk surface should ideally be slanted 20 degrees** toward the child.

The **proper height** of the seat is also very important, and when sitting in upright posture, your child should be able to place both feet flat on the floor. Children who have restless or cold feet often like sticking their feet into a big pillowcase filled with a soft and warm pillow or other material. This gives them support and warmth while they are working at their desk.

Most children with symptoms of visual stress tend to shorten their sight distance to the book or writing surface drastically. Some children even put their head on the desk to reduce the distance from their eyes to the work surface to less than 4 inches. It is simply impossible for anyone to see well at that distance.

Children suffering from problems with binocular vision often unconsciously position their body in a way that allows temporary relief for their eyes by actively interrupting their binocular vision and looking at things with one eye only. For example, they may turn their head to the side, keep a very short distance to the writing surface or book, put their head on their arm, or even **cover one of their eyes** with one hand. Thus, when you see your child again and again holding a hand over one eye while doing homework or turning the head in an unnatural way while reading or writing, this can indicate that binocular vision may be stressful for your child. Rather than interpreting your child's behavior as ill-mannered and bad posture, understand that this is an unconscious attempt to make better seeing possible. Of course this goal is not achievable this way.

In certain instances a child may have an ocular condition such as nystagmus, Duane's Syndrome, or ocular torticollis in which a special head or body posture is adopted to maintain the best vision. This is why it is crucial to consult with a developmental optometrist who can provide guidance on the functional implications of these conditions. Some of these children may benefit from yoked prism prescriptions to reposition their work space relative to their head or body position.

The **optimal distance for near work**, such as reading and writing, can be measured reliably for everyone with a built-in "yardstick" that is part of our body – namely, our forearm. Specifically, the proper distance for near work, called the **Harmon distance**, after the American optometrist Dr. Darrel Boyd Harmon who discovered this in his experiments, is equal to the length of your forearm from fist to elbow. That is, when you hold a fist under your chin, your elbow should touch your desk or work surface.

6.06

ENDING THE HOMEWORK DRAMA: HOW TO CREATE RELAXED CONDITIONS FOR YOU AND YOUR CHILD

For many stressed school children and their parents every afternoon brings a rerun of the drama brought on by the inevitable homework. Often kids are still tired from school, and because their power of judgment is not yet developed, they don't have an accurate picture of how high the pile of homework really is. Since children do not yet have a fully developed sense of time, they can easily feel overwhelmed and crushed by the mountain of work they feel is looming over them. They assume the work will take an endlessly long time and therefore will try to avoid the inevitable by postponing the work for as long as possible.

Of course, children need at least a 30-minute break or rest period after eating before they can work effectively. But after that time of rest, do not let your child haphazardly and grumpily wade into the homework pile without a plan. Do not wait with guidance and correction until after mistakes have been made. Instead, help your child plan and prepare the work before he or she begins with homework.

For example, before any homework task is started, sit down with your child to discuss what must be done and to plan the work. Let your child tell you in detail what the assignments are. It is important that you leave this role to your child rather than take it on yourself, as you want your child to learn to work independently. It is most helpful to talk over together beforehand what exactly your child's homework assignments are and then to develop together with the child a clear visual outline of the work to be done that day. Of course, in this process you should only assist. Allow your child to do the planning and to assess whether he or she is up to the task, what materials are needed, what questions must still be resolved, and what additional information must be gathered before work can begin.

Children usually have homework assignments in several subject fields, and it is therefore helpful to subdivide the pile of homework into several smaller hills. For example, after discussing the tasks, the necessary materials for homework in English, Math, or General Studies can be sorted into differently colored baskets; that way children can have a much clearer overview of their homework.

For assignments that are more complex and involve several steps that must be completed in sequence it is helpful to draw up a roadmap or itinerary during the planning phase. This plan can be placed on the desk, and your child can then check off each of the steps as it is completed.

It will also be very helpful if you can do a brief visualization exercise with your child with both of you envisioning how your child will work, what the completed work will look like, and the good feeling your child will have when he or she can put the first basket with a completed task aside. Some children find it very motivating to imagine what they will do as a reward in the brief break after one task is finished and before tackling the next.

Your child can then begin to do the homework by taking the contents of the first basket to the desk on which there is nothing else that could be distracting. When that task is done, the basket with all its contents can then be removed from the desk. By placing the baskets with work still to be done on the left side of the desk and the ones with work already completed on the right side, your child can always have a clear overview of his or her remaining workload and progress.

This visual and palpable segmentation of the work into smaller portions is very helpful for many children. Once the afternoon's homework is prepared and structured into work steps, it is best that you as parent step away and let your child work independently until the task agreed on has been completed. Some children prefer when you review their work with them. Others hate the process of review and correction so much that you should clearly discuss and agree in advance with your child and his or her teachers whether and how to review homework. Some teachers actually prefer seeing what the child has accomplished on his or her own without corrective input from a parent.

As you plan the homework together with your child, do not neglect to plan the necessary breaks. Many parents and even many teachers make the mistake of basing their planning on their own power of concentration. However, elementary school children can maintain sustained visual concentration for about 20 minutes at most before it flags considerably. And when children have visual problems, their visual performance declines much sooner. By taking this into account you are practicing what is called "visual hygiene". This is when you help your child to manage or reduce stress that could otherwise occur from overloading the visual system. Think of it as avoiding sensory overload, which is a great strain on children and particularly detrimental for a child who may have generalized sensory integration or sensitivity problems.

It is best to include brief breaks during which your child can get up from the desk for a short time, stretch a bit, get something to drink, and perhaps even let the gaze roam out the window to rest his or her eyes by looking at something green in nature. During such breaks your child could also do the eye relaxation exercises learned in visual therapy. When all the homework is done, looking at the work baskets that have been moved from left to right will bring home to everyone how much has been achieved.

Sustained concentration span of children:

→ **5–7 years:** on average 10–15 minutes

→ **7–10 years:** on average 15–20 minutes

→ **10–12 years:** on average 20–25 minutes

→ **12–14 years:** on average 30 minutes

A-ha!

Chapter

Therapy for Disorders of Visual Functions and Processing

7

THERAPY
FOR DISORDERS OF VISUAL FUNCTIONS AND PROCESSING

7.01

LAURA'S DISORDER OF VISUAL FUNCTIONS AND PROCESSING

In chapter 3 you met Laura and learned about her problems in school, her recurring fatigue after simple learning tasks, and her frequent headaches. Laura was suffering from the typical symptoms of undiagnosed disorders of visual functions and processing. The diagnostic process lasted about three hours and revealed that Laura's learning problems were caused by a disorder in her binocular visual functions.

Laura's monocular visual acuity for letters and numbers at 20 feet was excellent, but at near vision range she could not see clearly with both eyes at the same time. A **deficit in her accommodative flexibility** – that is, in her autofocus function – caused her to see things blurry for several seconds when she looked up from her book to the blackboard about 13 feet away. In books, she sometimes saw double letters or, as a result of intermittent suppression, lines or parts of letters disappeared altogether for a short moment so that she could not see the details of letters or words clearly. At other times

220

this resulted in instability of print, the confusion and visual discomfort one might experience when trying to read in a moving car. In special testing of her eye muscle function Laura had to guide little blue crosses to cover little red points, wearing red and blue glasses. She always landed a few inches next to the measuring point even though she felt she had hit the target exactly. This type of examination is called coordimetry, and it provides a measurement of how accurately both eyes work together as a team. The test showed that Laura had a significant weakness in the control and guidance of her external eye muscles (m. recti mediales), the convergence muscles of both eyes. This muscle dysfunction is known as convergence insufficiency (CI).

The convergence near point, the point when both convergence muscles reach maximum range, should be at a distance from the object of about 2-3 inches. However, when Laura tried to look with both eyes at a point 10 inches

INTERMITTENT CENTRAL SUPPRESSION (ICS) – SUPPRESSION EFFECTS IN READING

When fusion fails, there are only two ways for our brain to respond to images that do not match perfectly: we will either see two images in different places – that is, we will have double vision – or our brain temporarily switches off or suppresses the image that is misaligned.

away for 3 seconds, one eye kept sliding outward. She was diagnosed with convergence insufficiency combined with intermittent central suppression. In other words, her visual cortex blocked out parts of the misaligned images momentarily. That is why she unconsciously sometimes covered one of her eyes with her hand to avoid the irritation of double vision, which occurred only when she was using both eyes at the same time.

Laura had no stable fusional capacity and significantly reduced fusional ranges combined with deficits in stereoscopic or 3D vision. In addition to this, her ability to move her eyes horizontally, needed for fluent reading, was at the level of a five-year-old preschooler.

When she had to assess the spatial orientation of letters, Laura was sometimes uncertain and continued to confuse "b" and "d" when reading. This is a problem kids typically overcome by the time they reach the second half of first grade. Laura's ability to perceive words and letter combinations correctly with one look, her span and speed of **simultaneous visual perception** was measured at **three letters in 800 milliseconds**. In contrast, children who read well can quickly recognize as many as six letters in 100 milliseconds. **Laura was eight times slower at perceiving half as many letters as her peers.**

Infrared oculography is a reading measurement that tracks eye movements by means of infrared cameras and revealed a significant impairment in the coordination of Laura's eye muscle functions and reading saccades. The cameras showed an excessive number of regressions, involuntary movements

HER READING SPEED WAS
23 WORDS / MINUTE INSTEAD OF
120 WORDS / MINUTE.

from right to left, in the opposite direction to the flow of reading, that runs from left to right. Essentially, these movements slowed Laura down and were a source of frustration because she frequently lost her place, skipped a line, and had to rediscover the word just read. Depending on the length of words she was trying to read, Laura had to look at them not just once but three or four times in order to locate and identify the word. Her reading speed was equally slow at **only 23 words per minute**. The average speed for children her age is 95 to 120 words per minute. In other words, Laura had to exert a lot of effort to navigate texts with her eyes. **Reading a text for the first time, she could comprehend less than 30 percent of the content she had to read everything several times to understand it.** Instead of allocating her attentional resources towards reading fluency and comprehension, she had to spend them on the effort to maintain a clear, single, and stable printed image.

Like vision itself, Optometric Vision Therapy is based on learning processes

Vision is an innate brain function but an ability our brain learns in a process that begins in the early phases of embryonic development. As soon as the newborn opens its eyes, a process of recognition, understanding, and learning begins and continues throughout life.

Our brain is a kind of learning computer that is never inactive at any time in our life. Even when we are sleeping, our brain is not set to standby mode but is intensely busy processing the perceptions and experiences we have gathered in our waking state. At the same time our sense of hearing remains alert to any suspicious noises.

Every conscious perception that is repeated leaves traces in our brain. These traces then connect through neural networks in the nervous system with other perceptual functions and with our ability to remember, to speak, and to think. Thus our perceptions for learning are utilized at multiple levels all time.

Francis Crick who was awarded the Nobel Prize for his discovery of the molecular structure of DNA also closely studied biological aspects of visual consciousness and described its function as follows:

The biological purpose of visual consciousness in human beings is to provide the best possible interpretation of visual perceptions in light of prior experiences, which can be ones the individual has had or can comprise older experiences embedded in the individual's genes. To make this interpretation available long enough to that part of the brain that plans and initiates the essential motor output in the form of actions or speaking we need the functions of the working memory. Clearly, the term "visual consciousness" thus covers a variety of sensorimotor processes.

In Optometric Vision Therapy we raise our patients' awareness of their visual functions, which take up such a large part of the brain and are intimately connected to our consciousness, intelligence, and ability to learn. With specially designed and individualized exercises, Vision Therapy helps patients gain deliberate control of these crucial functions of perception and processing.

7.02
WHAT HAPPENS IN OUR BRAIN WHEN WE ARE LEARNING?

For our brain, learning means the development of new interconnections between neural pathways and the formation of processing patterns. Neural pathways connect individual neurons called nerve cells. An adult's brain consists of about 100 billion of such neurons that communicate with other neurons via more than 100 trillion contact points, the synapses. When we open our eyes, our **vision accounts for the stunning amount of about two-thirds of the brain's electrical activity**. This is a full 2 billion of the 3 billion firings per second – a discovery made by the neuroanatomist R. S. Fixot first published in a paper in 1957.

At birth, an infant's brain has the same number of neurons as that of an adult; however, a baby's brain weighs only a quarter of an adult's. The newborn's neurons are not yet fully formed and not yet widely or fully interconnected. In infants and toddlers each individual neuron initially has fifteen times as many synapses as the neurons in an adult's brain. This allows for a huge number of connections, but in the long run only the **most important ones that are used successfully** will remain. Interestingly, as the brain matures, **the number of options decreases** in favor of **energy-saving, efficient, and automated inter-connections** and networks. This neural pruning occurs at every level of the central nervous system.

As nerve fibers and their supporting sheath of glia cells grow, the fibers become thicker, and the volume of the brain increases. In the process, the transport of information is stabilized and accelerated. Each neuron is connected with many other neurons through a protrusion called axon. These connections can vary in length from fractions of a hundredth of an inch to more than 3 feet. The total length of all neural pathways in an adult's brain amounts to **about 4,000 miles**, which is **145 times the circumference of the earth**.

Separating the Wheat from the Chaff

At every moment a vast number of impressions and perceptions is flowing from our body via the senses to our brain. Not all of these perceptions and learning experiences can or should be stored in the brain. Rather, a selection is made, **sorting out what is important** from what is unimportant, and perceptions are organized into **categories and patterns**. Our brain integrates impressions into **meaningful sequences**, establishes relationships to other perceptual experiences, and amends knowledge that has already been stored with new information as it is learned. Neurons that are frequently used and have multiple strong interconnections among each other are maintained while connections not used as much are dismantled physically.

While we are asleep, perceptual content is consolidated. For instance during the Rapid Eye Movement (REM) phase of sleep, our brain is actively processing the impressions gathered during the day. That is why babies need to sleep repeatedly during the day and get tired easily. Their brain is engaged in the intensive activity of expanding and interconnecting neural pathways. Many five-year-olds actually still need a nap around noontime or they will be drowsy, weepy, or cranky. Left without sufficient sleep, their cognitive performance will also decline.

7.03
NEUROPLASTICITY

As we have seen, learning is work for our brain, and quite literally construction work. **New experiences, perceptions, and impressions change the substance and architecture of the brain.** This ability of our brain to constantly "remodel" itself is called neuronal plasticity or neuroplasticity. Without that ability continuous learning would not be possible.

In fact, in the past 10 years brain research has refuted the notion that our brain's potential steadily and inexorably decreases as we age and that its established structures cannot be changed. Instead, neurons grow or change in response to injuries of neuronal tissue as well as react to changes in our environment, enabling us to adapt to them. This **neuroplasticity is the foundation of our ability to learn**. Both the functions and the physical structure of neurons or of entire brain areas can change. **We now know that with training stroke patients in their eighties can still create new cell connections in their brain.** These new connections can then take over functions that are limited or destroyed at other locations in the brain. For example, when right-handed persons have to use their left arm to take over for a broken right upper arm, they show distinctive and measurable changes in the motor regions of the brain governing the left arm after 16 days of using only the left arm.

This is not to discount the importance of early intervention and developmental experiences. The brain is definitely more plastic or malleable in youth. However, with determination and hard work on the part of patients, caretakers, and therapists, significant changes can still occur in adulthood even if perhaps not as readily as in childhood.

Recent studies show that frequent repetition of motor functions can affect the size of the brain. For example, in teenagers nowadays the motor cortex area that governs the thumbs is about three times larger than it was in teens in the 1970s. That is, frequent texting is also leading to brain training.

An experiment has confirmed that **mental activity and imagination also can increase the size of brain areas**. In that study, one group of students practiced a simple piece of music on the piano, and a second group merely visualized playing that piece on the piano. At the end of the study the subjects' corresponding brain areas were examined, and in the first group the area that governs finger motions had grown. Astonishingly, the very same brain areas had also increased in size in the second group that had only imagined the piano playing.

7.04
BIOFEEDBACK

Biofeedback (from bios = Greek word for "life") therapy is based on our ability to perceive the functions of our body and to learn to control them deliberately. Essentially, biofeedback therapy is a kind of learning therapy. Body functions we are usually not aware of must be made visible or audible and thus observable so that we can become aware of them. The goal of biofeedback therapy is to become able to control certain functions consciously and deliberately. For this purpose, body signals we usually cannot perceive consciously are measured and played back to us in the form of perceptible, visual and auditory stimuli.

In the 1960s it was discovered that it is possible to influence certain physiological functions, such as the regulation of blood flow in the skin or heart rate. These functions are controlled by the autonomic nervous system and had previously been thought not to be accessible to conscious control. Biofeedback therapy is based on the insight that **physiological reactions of our body can be influenced through feedback**, that is, through a conscious response. **When visual or digital signals make otherwise autonomous body functions observable, we can learn to bring them under the control of our will.**

For example, we can learn to slow down our heart rate deliberately. To make this possible, a pulse sensor displays a heart rate that is too fast in red on a screen or on a handheld device, and the slower desired or target frequency is represented in green. By deepening our breathing and relaxing our muscles, we can learn to change the red color gradually into green. With some practice, we can create and maintain this state for a longer period of time and keep the rate in the green area. Then the desired goal of slowing down the heart rate is achieved. Eventually, after practicing for some time, merely imagining the green signal can bring about the desired condition.

The goal of classic biofeedback therapy is to train conscious control of body functions so that ultimately even **a brief visualization of the desired process**

brings about the desired physiological change. For example, certain forms of headaches are accompanied by a muscle tension around the jaw joint. After the body function "muscle relaxation around the jaw joint" has been trained for some time with biofeedback therapy, even just a brief visualization of the desired process will help to relax the muscles in that area.

In the past few years new therapies aimed at controlling brain functions have been developed especially for children. With the so-called **neurofeedback training**, they learn to replace theta brainwaves, slow action potentials in the cerebral cortex that signal inattention, with beta activity, brain waves that go hand in hand with focused attention. These training methods are used primarily for children with attention deficit disorders (ADD). They can learn to control their brain activity, which is made observable by means of electro-encephalogram (EEG) monitoring in such a way that sustained attention becomes possible for them. In training sessions, children practice controlling the movements of objects displayed on a screen by using only their imagination and concentration. For example, children learn to use concentrated mental activity to maintain the flight altitude of a helicopter on a screen at a constant level. If their concentration wavers or decreases, the object sinks.

Visual information is the ideal stimulus for biofeedback and neurofeedback therapy and is also well suited to bring certain body or mental conditions to awareness. That is why many of these methods work with visual concentration, visualization, and visual feedback through colors or images on a computer screen.

7.05

VISUAL FEEDBACK – AN IMPORTANT FACTOR IN VISION THERAPY

When vision itself is the object of therapeutic intervention, then special conditions apply – after all, in that case our visual consciousness works with itself!

Vision is a process of perception that regulates itself and maintains its balance through sensorimotor control circuits. Just think of the accommodation-convergence reflex where sensory sensory information, such as a slight change in fixation distance causing images to be less sharp, triggers autonomous reflexes that immediately activate the ciliary muscles, adjusting and increasing the refractive power of the lenses. At the same time, the external eye muscles provide the convergence movement in accordance with the fixation distance.

Vision training works by making patients aware of various **components** of these sensorimotor control circuits. In this process, visual key stimuli provide **feedback about a function's condition** and at the same time strengthen the sensory or motor components of vision.

Specially designed and constructed therapy materials facilitate direct visual feedback regarding the visual-neurophysiological functions to be worked on. For example, after the retina has been exposed to a flash of light in the shape of a line or stripe, the afterimage, which persists for a few minutes, makes the fixation positions of the eyes visible in space. When so-called anaglyph glasses are used, the patient's left eye looks through a green lens and the right eye through a red one. This separation of colors makes feedback possible and allows the patient to become aware of which eye perceives which visual stimulus. Similar effects are obtained with polarized glasses you may be familiar with from 3D movies. Since each eye sees only one half of the picture presented, patients can become aware of double images and of the effect of the suppression function. When both eyes are used together properly, the depth sensation is much greater than when either eye is viewing independently.

Visual material that includes **control characters** allows feedback regarding the stability of binocular perception. For example, a picture of a magician looks the same for both eyes, but the left eye sees him wearing a hat while the right eye sees him without hat but with a magic wand in his hand. Children with stable binocular vision see the figure with both attributes, hat and magic wand, at the same time. If suppression is involved, the hat or wand disappears sometimes and becomes visible again a short time later.

In another technique different **lenses or prisms** are used to create a blurry image that supports a desired sensorimotor effect. For example, a stimulation or relaxation of accommodation and convergence through minus or plus lenses. Indirect signals, such as **acoustic signals**, can also be used to make patients aware of any deviation from the correct position of their gaze. Many of our computer-based therapy programs use auditory stimuli in order to give patients feedback on correct or incorrect viewing and fusion positions.

Visual or auditory feedback can also support exercises for improving eye-hand coordination and balance. For example, an electronic pen can emit a beep to indicate the slightest deviation from the ideal graphomotor position. Balancing boards can indicate visually on a monitor every deviation from a desired gross motor pattern that requires balance and coordination. Direct visual feedback can also be generated through animated 3D images that are used as stimuli for maintaining convergent and divergent fusion. In addition, infrared cameras allow direct monitoring of gaze positions as a patient is reading a text. One of the original applications of biofeedback in Optometric Vision Therapy was auditory biofeedback for eye movement control in nystagmus. By listening to a tone that became softer as eye movement jitter decreased, patients learned to reduce this oscillation on a voluntary basis. In other words, they were able to bring eye movement under voluntary control and stabilize it even in a condition that was previously thought to be completely involuntary and uncontrollable.

The therapist has to decide which type of feedback to use, and in which phase of the therapy based on the material characteristics and the patient's abilities and limitations. The concept guiding the therapy is always based on activity. That is, the doctor does not simply prescribe something for the patient, and the patient is not just a passive recipient of eye glasses or gets one of his eyes covered with a patch. On the contrary. Optometric Vision Training works with top-down processes. Patients learn consciously and actively to use training methods that help them monitor and control their visual functions. Among other things, patients learn:

→   How and where to **direct** their gaze

→   How to **analyze** and understand what they have seen

→   How to **control** their conscious perception in such a way that they can always see well in every direction and at any distance

→   How to **apply** the necessary adjustments in their daily life and in learning situations

---

This type of learning requires understanding the process. When working with children a dialog is necessary to inform them about the purpose and significance of the exercises in a way they can understand. **Well-informed children who understand what their problem is and how they can solve or overcome it are usually very successful in their vision training.** It is always inspiring to see that even children as young as 7 years old can understand their therapy and commit themselves to it when they are taken seriously as team partners in the therapeutic process.

It is especially helpful to agree on a **goal that is important and meaningful to the child**. These goals can be formulated as very concrete wishes. For example, a child may say:

→ **I want** to able to read correctly.

→ **I want** to be able to finish reading an entire book all the way to the end.

→ **I don't want** to not have headaches anymore when I come home from school.

Or:

→ **I want** to be goalkeeper and catch balls.

→ **I want** to learn to hit the balls and beat my brother in a tennis match.

Even a seven year old child can understand that these abilities are closely connected to the ability to see well.

Of course, parents also must have a clear understanding of the therapy's goals. Their cooperation in the therapeutic process is essential because Optometric Vision Therapy works with visual brain functions and depends on doing eye exercises every day for about 10-15 minutes. Continuing with these exercises in a disciplined way at home is essential to success. Only with regular repetition the new abilities will be securely anchored and eventually become automatic. Good and productive cooperation at home between the child and his or her adult caregivers is indispensable. In most cases, mothers are the ones who work with the child at home, but we have also seen very successful therapies involving a child's father or grandparents as part of the team.

It is quite an achievement and indeed a high art to maintain the discipline for daily work on a child's perceptual problems amid a stressful daily life and in addition to the usual pile of homework along with the child's continuing poor performance in school. We have the utmost respect for the team of caregiver, child, and therapist for their team effort in making Vision Therapy successful.

7.06
THERAPY FOR A CONVERGENCE PROBLEM

Optometric Vision Therapy includes numerous and varied therapy activities. Accordingly it takes years of training to understand them and be able to use them appropriately. Every patient has different abilities and limitations, so the therapy process has to be customized specifically for each patient. Therapy plans are never identical. This makes the description of a typical therapy difficult. The following example of Laura's therapy for convergence insufficiency can serve to illustrate underlying concepts and approach.

As described above in more detail, convergence insufficiency develops when the eye muscles cannot be properly controlled to allow the axes of both eyes to be turned inward, which is necessary for both eyes to focus on the same spot in near vision. This convergence position must be maintained consistently for longer periods of time without the eyes getting tired. It is only when children can use this function easily and without complaining of tiredness that they can work comfortably for longer periods of time in near vision range, the same range used for reading, writing, or solving arithmetic problems.

CYBERNETIC MODEL OF PERFECT VISION

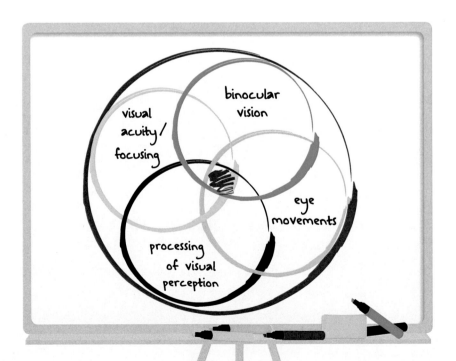

When children do not have this ability, their eyes keep sliding away from the targeted convergence position toward the outside. As a result, they lose focus, briefly see double or through suppression lose binocular vision. Constantly having to work with eye muscles that are not functioning correctly is very tiring. Naturally, children then cannot fully concentrate on their task; they make more mistakes, and effectiveness and performance decline.

Ophthalmologists often do not address convergence issues at all, and when they do, they usually recommend pencil push-ups. The instructions for this exercise are as follows: "Hold a pencil about 12 inches in front of your nose and then push it closer and closer toward your nose. And all the while keep your eyes on the tip of the pencil. If you do this exercise every day for 10 minutes, your eye muscles will get stronger."

However, for most children with convergence problems this exercise is painful because it demands something that their muscles cannot do. Getting children with convergence insufficiency to do this exercise correctly even for only two minutes is nearly impossible. Instead, it makes more sense to include in the therapy process all functional aspects that are involved in convergence movements. Since they are part of a complex reflex sequence involving the accommodation-convergence reflex, the individual components can be worked on and improved separately at first and can then be re-integrated.

For Laura it was therefore useful to work monocular initially, that is, with one eye only, to train acuity and accommodative flexibility and thus the activity of her ciliary muscles and lenses. In addition, she had to learn how to accurately localize objects in space and to match spatial localization in the right eye with that in the left eye. For this, a feedback process was used for each eye separately.

In this process, plus and minus lenses called flippers, are used alternately. Minus lenses activate the accommodative response while plus lenses have a relaxing effect. These lenses are used for alternately looking at writing or images in various sizes at various distances. Through the deliberate, conscious use of accommodative functions the patient learns how to make the artificially "blurred" image sharp again. This requires deliberately increasing the accommodative muscle tone or using a so-called soft gaze that relaxes the muscle tone of the ciliary muscle. In other words, the sharpness of the image serves as key stimulus for the desired state of accommodation. A detailed description of combinations of this exercise with convergence and fusional activities goes beyond the scope of this book.

In this context, it is important to mention that convergence and other vision problems involving the eye muscles can also arise when people are particu-

MARSDEN BALL EXERCISE

larly tense and have tight, clenched muscles in and around the eyes. In those cases, it is helpful for patients to learn relaxing breathing techniques. These breathing techniques transmit the necessary impulse to the autonomic nervous system, which plays a significant role in controlling the eyes' autofocus.

Once the accommodating activity can be successfully carried out at a given distance, the training exercises can be made more challenging for the patient by requiring movement and changing the viewing distance. For example, Laura found it especially difficult to carry out tasks that involved shifts in viewing distance, like when she had to look at things close up and then something else some distance away. For example, in therapy she practiced to read three numbers at a distance of about 13 feet and then the next three numbers at 16 inches; her eyes had to carry out tasks. The rapid change of focus and the oculomotor task of searching and orientation, both require intense concentration. The function of repeated practice is to turn a conscious control process into something more reflexive in nature and to build automaticity.

At first, such exercises are practiced with only one eye because the brain initiates each movement by sending equally strong impulses to the muscles of both eyes at the same time. Even while working with one eye only, the patient's whole ocular motor system is involved. When a child has mastered these tasks and can easily change focus and fixation with one eye, then we move on to the next level, involving binocular vision. In binocular exercises the child must deliberately coordinate the muscles of both eyes so that convergence is produced and can be maintained.

We begin training this with an exercise including a swinging Marsden ball, which was already used in monocular training to practice fixation and functions of the oculomotor system. Now we train the binocular movements needed for tracking an object; as they track the ball the children at the same time must read the numbers and letters on it. Alternatively, we may use this exercise to improve eye-hand coordination. The ball swings back and forth, which means that more or less convergence is needed to fix the gaze on it as the ball moves. The child's task here is to track the ball's movement and in the right moment to tap specified points on the ball with a colored stick.

To achieve secure and reliable convergence we need to have effective fusion, that is, we must be able to fuse the images from the two eyes readily into one visual impression, at any distance and regardless of the direction in which we're looking at the moment. Fusion training is therefore a central concern of Optometric Vision Therapy and accordingly was a major component of Laura's therapy for convergence insufficiency.

If visual acuity is poor in one eye or if one eye is not perfectly integrated into the binocular perception process – for example, if the left eye's perception is often switched off through intermittent central suppression ICS) – then anti-suppression exercises or exercises for monocular fixation in a binocular field (MFBF training) must be practiced before any other therapy can be started. MFBF therapy works with the anaglyph glasses described above that allow for a separation of the right eye's perceptions from those of the left eye by means of color. To increase the patient's awareness of the eye with unstable perceptual functions, this eye's perceptions can be enhanced during the exercises while those of the other eye are deliberately dimmed through filters or colored overlays.

Practicing with Physiological Double Images

To help patients develop an awareness of fixation, distance, and binocular perception it is useful to work with the Brock String. This ingeniously simple tool got its name from Dr. Frederick W. Brock, an American optometrist, and is essentially a piece of string with three or more small or large beads in different colors placed at various distances along the string. The string serves as a kind of visual axis in space, and the arrangement of the beads allows the patient to practice and experience convergence and spatial perception in a continuum along this inward/outward axis.

The Brock string is also a useful tool for perceiving and understanding the phenomenon of physiological double images or physiological diplopia. Here, the child is instructed to focus on one of the balls and at the same time, with a sort of **divided attention**, to activate perception in the peripheral visual field. Soon the child will realize that all areas of the string that are not in focus are seen as double images – a phenomenon we are not aware of in our ordinary, every-day seeing. This is why some parents of children who are diagnosed with having inattention or ADHD report that after their child has mastered a technique such as the Brock String, the child's ability to control his or her visual attention has improved considerably.

BROCK-STRING-TRAINING

Perceiving this physiological diplopia requires that our binocular vision is stable and reliable. At the beginning of her therapy, Laura achieved this only for a short time and only at a distance of about 6 feet. At the end of her successful fusion therapy she only had to imagine a point on the visual axis at a distance of about 3 inches in order to physically focus on that point and at the same time activate maximum peripheral vision. She was eventually able to vary each convergence position at will.

Special exercises were used to work with Laura on her spatial or 3D vision, which is the highest level of binocular vision. These exercises use 3D images, such as objects in space, computer simulations, and special therapy apps on a tablet PC. After a few weeks, Laura's impaired stereo vision normalized through this therapy.

Computer Assisted Training

There are many computer programs for training various aspects of visual perception, including convergence, fusion, fusional ranges, and 3D vision. We used them often in certain phases of therapy, and Laura liked them very much. However, her visual abilities must work reliably and correctly in her daily life with and without a computer's visual demands. Therefore, the core of our therapy was devoted to exercises in "natural" as opposed to virtual spaces. Of course, the way our society is evolving, having efficient visual skills for sustained computer use is becoming progressively more important.

7.07
AN IMPORTANT PHASE:
TURNING LEARNED SKILLS INTO SECOND NATURE

In the beginning her training required Laura's complete concentration, and she was not always successful in doing the exercises. However, as soon as she was able to do them more reliably and became more confident, we worked with her on automatization. This is when the initially difficult tasks had to become automatic so Laura could carry them out confidently, reliably, and in a relaxed way. It is only when these abilities become second nature, that we can begin the last phase of therapy.

All the individual visual components practiced in Vision Therapy are basic functions for working successfully on visual tasks. These functions must be stable, reliable, and consistent so the patient can do additional activities. It is not enough that children can develop and maintain stable convergence in the therapy session. In the **loading phase**, we make the visual task much more difficult by adding other activities that require concentration, thinking, and talking.

For example, it was a great challenge for Laura to maintain convergence, which had been insufficient before her therapy, and at the same time solve an arithmetic problem, spell out words backwards, or summarize a text. Laura had to practice convergence with divided attention and in combination with other activities until she could reliably achieve this successfully. Only then were we sure that Laura had mastered these abilities and would be able to call on them any time in stressful situations in school.

Since Laura panicked easily, this was a great challenge. While doing her visual exercises in therapy, she had to imagine stressful situations and practice not getting distracted, but remaining focused on her task, and accomplish it with perfection. It took her a few weeks to be reliably successful in achieving this goal in even the most difficult exercises and under very stressful conditions.

Disorders of Visual Functions and Processing Typically Occur in Combination

Isolated disorders of convergence are a relatively rare phenomenon in school children. Most of the children we diagnose and treat have several vision problems that can include all conceivable combinations of the perceptual disorders discussed in chapter 4 on diagnostics. Likewise, Laura suffered not only from a convergence insufficiency. Our diagnostic process led to the following findings:

Laura had a convergence problem and exophoria combined with difficulties in recognizing the spatial orientation of letters and numbers, very slow simultaneous visual processing for letter combinations, problems in controlling her horizontal eye movements, and extremely slow reading speed compared to the average for children her age.

Describing the entire process of such a complex therapy clearly goes beyond the scope of this book. Fact sheets on Optometric Vision Therapy from the American Optometric Association show that the duration of therapy has to be extended when there are multiple visual factors compounding each diagnosis.

The brief description above of some basic therapy details should give you an idea of how Optometric Vision Therapy deals with very complex issues that affect all neurophysiological and neuropsychological components of vision. More detailed information can be found in textbooks dedicated to Optometric Vision Therapy, such as **Applied Concepts in Vision Therapy** by Dr. Leonard Press.

7.08
THE LAST PHASE OF THERAPY: APPLYING NEW SKILLS IN SCHOOL

Vision Therapy usually takes at least several months and in complex cases can take more than a year. In the last phase of therapy, in conversations with the child, we assess together whether the personal goal the child formulated at the beginning has been reached. If the goal has not been achieved, we talk about what else we can do to reach that goal. Having a goal of their own and participating in the process of deciding which abilities they want to develop will enhance children's self-esteem. Choosing their own goals and freely committing to doing the necessary work and training is an important developmental step for all youngsters. Children become able to master this step when they have experienced in the course of their Vision Therapy that they can overcome their difficulties by their own efforts. In this context, it is important that children know which skill area they are working on in their Vision Therapy and for which reason. They need to know what results they can expect, and such results should be measurable and quantifiable.

Once the basic visual functions have been learned and practiced, the new abilities must become automatic or second nature so that the child can easily and reliably use them in his or her everyday school life even when under stress and distracted. Accordingly, we check whether the new abilities are successfully **transferred** and can be **applied** as the child deals with the demands of school.

In most cases, children who started therapy because they suffered "only" from a physical visual disorder are completely free of their medical symptoms after several months of Vision Therapy. Now no longer having to struggle with persistent headaches, burning and hurting eyes, double vision, and related physiological problems, these children can successfully complete the tasks that used to be so difficult for them.

For example, children's handwriting often improves significantly after Vision Therapy and is neater and more easily legible due to improved visually guided fine motor control. Children also read more fluently and with increasing competence and energy due to improved visual scan paths for reading. Because their functioning visual spell scanner now more effectively connects the visual word image areas of the brain with the frontal eye fields in selective attention, these children also make fewer spelling errors.

In Laura's case, she started therapy when she was in second grade, and after eight months of therapy summarized her results in these words:

*"Before Vision Therapy I simply could not do my homework at all because after school my head and eyes hurt so much that I had to lie down. Doing my homework sometimes took three hours, and my mummy and I were in a bad mood all afternoon. Now, doing my homework takes only half an hour, and I can do it all by myself, and I have no headaches anymore. Before, **I really could not do my homework at all!** Now I sometimes **don't feel like doing my homework**, but that's a different matter!"*

Of course, the earlier Vision Therapy is started, the easier it is. Children who begin therapy as they start their school years only have to work on basic visual functions to step into the world of correct reading and writing. However, children who had to do their school work for years while hampered by an undetected vision problem will face a more complicated situation. For children already in third or fourth grade and used to working on tasks for which they are ill-equipped, the result described above is not necessarily the typical outcome.

Even Laura needed **special training in reading technique**. Children suffering for many years from undetected visual disorders that limit their achievements usually develop their own learning strategies and adaptations like **guessing strategies**. This learned behavior is not easily given up even after successful Vision Therapy.

Older Children Need Help to Change their Reading Behavior

Many children with serious reading disorders have years of practice in **guessing** rather than reading. Because of their perception disorder, guessing was the only way for them to meet the requirements of school to some extent, and older children have practiced guessing for several years out of necessity. Since they still tend to panic easily when having to read, these kids usually continue to use the learned and familiar technique even though, after Vision Therapy, they can now see and read perfectly well. Even when their optometric tests show perfect results in all measurements that compare performance before and after therapy, children do not automatically use their new abilities in school or when doing homework. For some children it is very difficult to give up **guessing, a technique they've practiced for years**, and instead using their perfect vision abilities also in reading and writing. This impediment to correct reading must be overcome; otherwise these children's school achievements will not improve despite their excellent technical results in vision training.

If children are dealing with such problems, they receive additional individualized Vision Therapy that focuses on the link between visual and cognitive issues. For example, if children have difficulties with math, we work with them on developing **visual-spatial perception and visualization and on visual perception of quantities**. When children have weaknesses in visual memory and problems with **grasping and memorizing word images**, we use special techniques to help them develop this visual ability. If a child's learning problem is primarily due to a pure reading disorder, we teach and practice reading techniques that are adapted to the specific problem. Many children who complete vision therapy with technically perfect visual functions and processing then begin "all on their own" to enjoy reading. However, if this is not the case, reading training that is especially adapted to a child's needs by a reading specialist is indispensable.

In very difficult cases we work temporarily with a "foreign" typeface, showing the child a text in one of the lesser known foreign languages, such as Finnish, Hungarian, or Turkish. Since children do not expect that they can read these foreign languages, their self-imposed pressure to succeed at reading falls away. Since no one else in the family can read that language either, children's panic diminishes soon. They relax and can learn to read exactly what is on the page. Of course, this method is only a brief transition stage to help children overcome the emotional problems hampering their reading by having a little fun. The big goal is to enable children to read aloud in their own language, fluently and with proper emphasis.

In the last phase of Vision Therapy we work with the children on **accelerating their reading speed** and also on **improving their reading comprehension**. As a result, children will learn to grasp what a text says as quickly and as accurately as possible. For some children, a technical **improvement in their visual simultaneous perception** is "all" that is needed to increase their reading speed. Other children need to be shown how the **"movie in the mind"** develops and how they can deliberately use and improve their ability to visualize.

Children who have struggled for years with vision problems often have poor technical reading skills and also a poor emotional relationship to reading. Many passionately summarize this in the words:

"I HATE READING!"

SIMULTANEOUS VISUAL PERCEPTION TRAINING

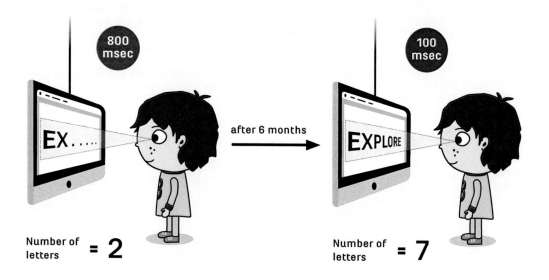

These kids associate stress and negative feelings with the process of reading, and it usually takes a while before they gradually notice that the formerly hated activity of reading now is actually easy and even fun. For some, this realization comes when they consciously experience their mastery of reading skills.

One of the most gratifying outcomes of our therapy program was achieved by a child who was in seventh grade when he started Vision Therapy. During the diagnostic reading test, this boy had debated about how many sentences he would be willing to read aloud, two or as many as three. After Vision Therapy he was reading with enthusiasm and kept asking his parents for new books and other reading material. He even sent us a list of books he'd read on his own – a list that was several pages long.

7.09
ACTIVATING THE SPELLING SCANNER

If a child's main learning problem is poor spelling, we focus our Vision Therapy on practicing simultaneous visual perception so the child can deliberately apply that ability in reading. When simultaneous visual perception functions properly, children can **consciously and correctly perceive and scan in the printed word images** during the reading process. These accurately scanned and consciously perceived images of the printed words then form the basis of a large inventory of error-free word images stored in memory. Since the words are all spelled correctly in the printed text, this is a **time-saving and very efficient method for learning how to spell**. On this foundation of correctly scanned words children can then develop a kind of **"spelling dictionary in the mind"** that grows with every new word they read correctly.

SIGHT WORD
VOCABULARY

Being able to perceive word images accurately and quickly at one glance is also very helpful when learning foreign languages. Learning how to spell correctly in Spanish, French, or German, for example, requires visual precision and a sort of photographic memory.

When children study foreign languages in high school, they are usually told to memorize the vocabulary of a lesson but don't get much instruction on how to do this. Moreover, the spelling rules of other languages are usually not taught in detail either. Teachers assume that their students can quickly and without problems perceive word images at a glance. Students with excellent visual abilities can indeed manage to learn and memorize their vocabulary without further instruction, and at the same time they can memorize the correct spelling of the foreign words.

However, children who struggled in elementary school and are barely able to spell words in their own language, often spelling them phonetically and wrongly, will have trouble writing in a foreign language if they try to spell foreign words by ear, so to speak.

They might spell

Of course, when children have repeatedly misspelled a word and practically **engraved the incorrect spelling in their memory** over the years, it is not easy to delete the incorrect spelling and replace it with the correct one. This process takes a long time and requires a special pedagogical method, which is offered in remedial classes in schools or in private institutes offering remedial spelling instruction. Kids struggling with spelling can benefit from such remedial programs and successfully complete them once the basic perceptual requirements for learning have been firmly established. When children can see and memorize words properly and clearly, they can learn how to spell correctly.

7.10
CAN ADULTS BE AFFECTED, TOO?

Adults can also suffer from disorders of visual function and processing. For some people this struggle has been part of their daily life since childhood and all through their school years. Even as adults, many people read only what they absolutely have to read and have resigned themselves to getting tired quickly with certain activities.

Some people find reading or working on a screen more difficult after the onset of age-related farsightedness or presbyopia. When people have visual functions, such as convergence, that are already weak, working for hours on computer screens because the job requires it can make the problems worse and lead to considerable physical impairment.

The individuals affected then suffer from red, burning or aching eyes, headache, vision problems because of double images or suppression, and difficulty concentrating. Ophthalmologists diagnose these symptoms as asthenopia. In some cases, reading glasses will help alleviate the symptoms, but for people with weak convergence or fusion deficits glasses alone will not be sufficient. Such visual symptoms are important to consider from the point of view of occupational medicine and economy. It is not at all rare that adults have severe symptoms and may then have to change their occupation because they can no longer work all day on computer work stations.

Optometric Vision Therapy with adapted procedures and slightly different material can also be very helpful for adults, too. For example, in our practice we often see adult patients who are sent to us by holistic orthopedists. The reason for this is usually that in their screening these specially trained orthopedists have discovered that their patients' chronic headaches and misalignment of the cervical spine are perhaps caused not just by an orthopedic problem but also by a functional visual one.

Indeed, within a few months of Vision Therapy adults can better understand their visual system, become aware of the functions, and control them deliberately in such a way that they no longer have any symptoms. For example, Sue Barry, professor of neurobiology, describes her success in regaining her stereo vision engagingly and impressively in her book, "Fixing my Gaze." Sue Barry experienced strabismus early in childhood and as a result had lost stereoscopic or 3D vision, but she was able to regain it with Vision Therapy when she was in her forties. In her book she presents moving descriptions of what the world looks like when seen with and without stereoscopic 3D vision.

The renowned American optometrist Dr. Leonard Press, past president of COVD and author of many textbooks, articles, and blogs on the topic of developmental optometry, describes Optometric Vision Therapy in his book **Applied Concepts in Vision Therapy** as follows:

Optometric Vision Therapy can be defined as the art and science of developing visual abilities to achieve optimal visual performance and comfort. During VT patients gain greater understanding of and control over their visual abilities and then develop the capacity to efficiently apply these abilities to relevant tasks and activities. The goal of VT ist to develop visual abilities so that the patient can meet the visual demands of variable and complex situations with greater efficiency, endurance and economy of effort.

I see!

CONCLUSION

In this book you have met children who, despite being of normal intelligence, struggled with learning difficulties, were unable to read, and made many spelling errors. Their problems were not the kind of eyesight problems that are detected through the usual vision screenings in school or through pediatricians, and their learning problems were secondary rather than primary. A typical case was that of Mario. Right away in first grade he had difficulties with learning the letters of the alphabet. In his squiggly handwriting he wrote words with twisted letters and seemed not to understand how "that reading thing" works. Formerly a cheerful preschooler, Mario in a matter of months had become a desperate little boy who could not keep up in school. His parents had taken him to an ophthalmologist, who checked Mario's eyesight and found his visual acuity to be excellent – Mario had 20/20 vision. His parents then assumed – wrongly – that his learning problems had nothing to do with the boy's visual functions.

As you now know, learning problems such as the ones Mario struggled with are not caused by problems with visual acuity, ability to concentrate, or willingness to learn. The causes lie rather in disorders of auditory and visual functions and the processing of perceptions.

Mario's learning problems were caused by a disorder of visual perception of the graphical features of letters and numbers combined with a dysfunction in his eye-hand coordination and his simultaneous visual perception. Moreover, because of **deficits in his auditory and visual working memory**, Mario could not remember which letter represented which sound, and he often forgot the sequence of letters in the words he tried to spell out. Mario lacked several essential preconditions for learning to read and write. These developmental deficits became evident **after** he started school and had not been noticed in his preschool days.

David's story, like that of Mario, showed how difficult learning is for children with undiagnosed hearing and vision problems. David's life changed once his auditory and visual processing disorders were addressed and cleared up. Improvement in his visual functions and processing after just a few months of Vision Therapy made it possible for him to continue learning in his regular school.

Another typical case was that of Laura's. She began having problems with reading and writing in second grade, and her difficulties became so serious that by third grade they almost led to academic failure for Laura. As requirements of faster reading and correct spelling grew, Laura fell further and further behind. A grade D on a dictation exercise became normal for her even though she had been taking remedial spelling courses since second grade. She could not read properly and could not remember how to spell the words she had studied for a dictation exercise. She kept making more and more and often new spelling errors. Her grades in all subjects continued to worsen and the homework situation became increasingly agonizing for her and her parents. Even when she studied and practiced for hours, success eluded her, and she continued to fail. Laura frequently complained that she had headaches, and she believed she was just stupid.

Like Mario, Laura also had normal visual acuity and did not need glasses. **However, thorough examination showed that Laura's other visual functions were significantly impaired. A subtle latent outward drift of her eyes called exophoria combined with convergence insufficiency and problems with focusing and accommodation as well as deficits in her eye muscle functions made it difficult for Laura to control her eye movements while reading.** Laura's eyes "stumbled" when she read and sometimes she saw double. Her simultaneous visual perception and her visual memory were only as developed as those of a preschooler.

The physical and neurophysiological functions of the eyes and the connected neuropsychological aspects of visual information processing were described in such detail because only when we know about these details, we can really understand the connection between vision and learning. Once these problems are diagnosed, they can be addressed effectively and successfully with therapy. This therapy does not involve medications but instead consists of active training to develop and strengthen the missing or fragile components of perceptual functions. As you now know, vision is a very complex and important brain function, and is not innate. We learn and develop it throughout life. With Optometric Vision Therapy we can significantly improve our visual functions and processing in a precisely targeted way.

Thanks to the training provided by **Optometric Vision Therapy**, Laura overcame her convergence insufficiency and now has no more vision disorders when she reads and no more headaches. She now enjoys reading, has tripled her reading speed, and is working on correctly scanning and remembering words at a glance while she reads.

Our hope is that knowledge of these disorders, which affect so many children, will soon become widespread. The extent of the problem is obvious. **According to the National Assessment for Education Progress Report Card for 2015, only about a third of American fourth and eighth graders read at proficiency level or better.**

The American Parent-Teacher Association (PTA) estimates that about 10 million American students are suffering from undiagnosed vision problems and need help because their achievements in school lag far behind their potential.

In the United States, as well as in other countries, schools provide a number of accommodations and adaptations to help students with vision problems to learn and flourish. It is important that parents are well-informed and know where and how they can get help for their children. Pediatricians, teachers, psychologists, and therapists who can help children with specific learning disabilities complete special training and continuing education courses to acquire the necessary expertise and skills in their field. However, there is still very little interdisciplinary communication.

This book is intended as a contribution to this urgently needed interdisciplinary dialogue. A deeper understanding of the connections between the medical, neuropsychological, and pedagogical aspects of learning problems will help many children, open up new therapeutic options, increase children's joy for learning, and improve their educational opportunities.

A DEEPER UNDERSTANDING OF THE CONNECTIONS BETWEEN THE MEDICAL, NEUROPSYCHOLOGICAL, AND PEDAGOGICAL ASPECTS OF LEARNING PROBLEMS WILL HELP MANY CHILDREN OPEN UP NEW THERAPEUTIC OPTIONS, INCREASE CHILDREN'S JOY FOR LEARNING, AND IMPROVE THEIR EDUCATIONAL OPPORTUNITIES.

Recommended Reading

You can find additional scientific information about visual functions and related studies and research topics, on the website of **College of Optometrists in Vision Development (COVD)** at **www.covd.org**.

For further study you can consult **"Vision Therapy References, Research, and Scientific Studies"** at **www.visiontherapy.org/vision-therapy/vision-therapy-studies.html**.

The website of the **British Association of Behavioural Optometrists**, **www.babo.co.uk**, also offers detailed information about symptoms and frequency of visual dysfunctions in school children.

You can also find more detailed information, including lists of optometrists in your state, on the website of **the American Optometric Association, www.aoa.org.**

The AOA publishes Clinical Practice Guidelines on the following pertinent topics:
- Care of the Patient with Learning Related Vision Problems
- Care of the Patient with Amblyopia
- Care of the Patient with Accommodative and Vergence Dysfunction
- Care of the Patient with Strabismus: Esotropia and Exotropia

You find relevant articles and information regarding scientific studies in the following journals:
- Vision Development and Rehabilitation
- Optometry and Vision Science
- Optometry and Vision Development
- Journal of Optometry and Visual Performance
- Journal of Behavioral Optometry
- Optometry – Journal of the American Optometric Association
- Documenta Ophthalmologica
- JAMA Ophthalmology

You can begin your search with the following keywords:
- Accommodative disorders
- Visual information processing disorders
- Non-strabismic binocular disorders
- Amblyopia
- Ocular motility dysfunctions
- Reading and learning.

If you would like to read more about the following topics, the works listed below will get you started:

Neuropsychology and child development

Ayres, Jean: Sensory Integration and the Child, *Western Psychological Services, new edition 2005*

Carter, Rita: Mapping the Mind, *University of California Press, revised edition 2010*

Dehaene, Stanislas: The Number Sense: How the Mind Creates Mathematics, *Oxford University Press, revised and updated edition 2011.*

Duckman, Robert: Visual Development, Diagnosis and Treatment of the Pediatric Patient, *Lippincot, Williams and Wilkins 2006*

Eide, Brock and Fernette Eide: The Mislabeled Child: How Understanding Your Child's Unique Learning Style Can Open the Door to Success, *Hachette Books, 2006*

Furth, Hans and Harry Wachs: Thinking Goes to School: Piaget's Theory in Practice, *Oxford University Press, 1975*

Gesell, Arnold: Vision: Its Development in Infant and Child, *OEP Foundation 1998*

Getman, GN: How to Develop Your Child's Intelligence, *OEP Foundation 2000*

Goldstein, Bruce: Sensation and Perception, *Cengage Learning. Revised edition 2009*

Johnson, Katie: Red Flags for Elementary Teachers, *Tendril Press 2015*

Ratey, John: A User's Guide to the Brain: Perception, Attention, and the Four Theaters of the Brain, *Vintage, 2002*

Rosner, Jerome: Helping Children Overcome Learning Difficulties, *Walker Publishing Company 2000*

Visual perception

Crick, Francis and Christof Koch: Consciousness and Neuroscience, *Cerebral Cortex, 8, 1998*

Crick, Francis and Christof Koch: The Problem of Consciousness, *Scientific American, 10, 2002*

Hoffman, Donald: Visual Intelligence: How We Create What We See, *Norton, 2000*

Huxley, Aldous: The Art of Seeing, *Creative Arts Book Company, 3rd edition 1982*

Ings, Simon: A Natural History of Seeing: The Art and Science of Vision, *Norton, 2000*

Kandel, Eric: Principles of Neural Science, *McGraw-Hill, 5th edition 2012*

Milner, David and Mel Goodale: The Visual Brain in Action, *Oxford University Press, 2d edition 2006*

Palmer, Steven: Vision Science: From Photons to Phenomenology, *MIT Press, 1999*

Sacks, Oliver: The Mind's Eye, *Vintage Books / Random House 2010*

Reading

Dehaene, Stanislas: Reading in the Brain: The Science and Evolution of a Human Invention, *Viking, 2009*

Griffin JR, Christensen GN, Wesson M, Erickson G: Optometric Management of Reading Dysfunction, *OEP Foundation 2000*

Manguel, Alberto: A History of Reading, *Penguin Books, 1997*

Stein J, Kapoula Z: Visual Aspects of Dyslexia, *Oxford University Press 2012*

Wolf, Maryanne: Proust and the Squid: The Story and Science of the Reading Brain, *Harper Perennial, 2008*

Therapy for visual disorders

Barry, Susan: Fixing My Gaze: A Scientist's Journey into Seeing in Three Dimensions, *Basic Books, reprint edition 2010*

Benoit, Jillian and Benoit, Robin: How Vision Therapy Changed my Daughter's Life, *Brown Books Small Press 2013*

Birnbaum, Martin: Optometric Management of Nearpoint Vision Disorders, *OEP Foundation, 2008*

Caloroso, Elizabeth and Michael Rouse: Clinical Management of Strabismus, *Butterworth-Heinemann, 2d edition 2007*

Chang A, Yu X, Ritter S: Neurovision Rehabilitation Guide, *CRC Press 2016*

Gimenez, Pilar Vergara: Crossed and Lazy Eyes, Myths, Misconceptions and Truths, *OEP Foundation 2016*

Hellerstein, Lynn: See It. Say It. Do It! The Parent's & Teacher's Action Guide to Creating Successful Students & Confident Kids, *HiClear Publishing, 2010*

Padula, William: Neuro-Optometric-Rehabilitation, *OEP Foundation 2000*

Padula, W., Munitz, R., Magrun, M: Neuro-Visual Processing Rehabilitation – An Interdisciplinary Approach, *OEP Foundation 2012*

Press, Leonard: Applied Concepts in Vision Therapy, *OEP Foundation, 2008*

Rosen, Wendy Beth: The Hidden Link between Vision and Learning – Why Millions of Learning-Disabled Children are Misdiagnosed, *Rowman and Littlefield 2016*

Scheiman, Mitchell and Michael Rouse: Optometric Management of Learning-related Vision Problems, *Elsevier Health Sciences, 2006*

Scheiman, Mitchell and Bruce Wick: Clinical Management of Binocular Vision: Heterophoric, Accommodative, and Eye Movement Disorders, *Lippincott Williams & Wilkins, 3rd edition 2008*

Wider S, Wachs H.: Visual / Spatial Portals to Thinking, Feeling and Movement, *Profectum Foundation 2012*

Hearing and speech

Alderman, Loraine and Yvonne Capitelli: I Get It! I Get It! How John Figures It Out: One Boy's Journey and Triumph with Auditory Processing Disorder, *Stoelting Company, 2012*

Bellis, Teri: When the Brain Can't Hear: Unraveling the Mystery of Auditory Processing Disorder, *Atria Books, 2003*

Davis, Dorinne S.: The Cycle of Sound, *Sound Works Inc. 2015*

Heymann, Lois.: The Sound of Hope: Recognizing, Coping with, and Treating Your Child's Auditory Processing Disorder, *Ballantine Books, 2010*

Press, Leonard: Parallels between Auditory and Visual Processing, *OEP Foundation 2012*

read more ...

Glossary

Below are brief explanations to important terms used in the visual disorder discussion provided in this book .

• **Visual acuity** refers to the clarity of eyesight. It is a measurement of the resolution and minimum distance at which two visual objects are still seen as separate or distinct objects. Clinically, visual acuity is typically measured by the smallest size letter or object one can see on a standardized eye chart and for the average person, this corresponds to a spatial resolution of about 0.05 inches at a distance of about 16 feet .

• **Accommodation** refers to the autofocus function of the eyes. It is a vision reflex of the eyes that adjusts automatically to maintain a clear image or focus on an object at various distances. Due to this reflex, we can rapidly change our focus on an object without losing any sharpness or clarity irrespective of changing distances between ourselves and the object.

• **Accommodative flexibility** is the ability to change focus accurately and rapidly at various viewing distances. The aim is to achieve visual clarity when switching views between two objects, say a desk and a board. One's accommodative flexibility can be tested and trained clinically with plus and minus lens flippers.

• **Convergence** is an ability controlled by external eye muscles that enables us to turn both eyes simultaneously inward and towards each other. This in turn allows us to fixate on a point in our near vision range. It also allows us to concentrate visually on tasks in near vision range. For example, when writing and reading on worksheets, books, or computer / tablet screens.

- **Accommodation-convergence reflex** is a reflex that adjusts the eyes' axes based on the perceived image's sharpness. The axes of our eyes are thus adjusted to the distance of the object we are focusing on at the moment. Accommodation and convergence are important functions of near vision and must be balanced in order to achieve clear, single, and simultaneous binocular vision.

- **Convergence insufficiency (CI) or weakness** is a problem in coordinating eye movements for near vision. When we suffer from insufficient convergence, our eyes tend to deviate outward from the point we fixate. When reading, this can lead to blurry or double vision. At the same time, reading will feel like a great exertion, and we tire quickly because we have to keep correcting the "sliding away" of the visual axis with increased activity of the eye muscles.

- **Binocular vision** is the ability of the brain to process the images received from the two eyes. As each eye offers a view from a slightly different perspective, binocular vision works to simultaneously merge them into one image through fusion. This is what makes three-dimensional perception or stereoscopic vision (3D vision) possible.

- **Strabismus** is a misalignment in the visual axes in which both eyes are not aimed at the same point at the same time.

- **Amblyopia** is a reduced visual acuity that occurs in one eye and cannot be corrected by means of correctives lenses. Amblyopia may be caused by the squint position of one of the eye axes or through large differences in refractive power between the two eyes. The perception of a squinting eye or of the eye that has very poor image quality is then "switched off" or "blocked" by the brain through suppression. This results in disorders of the binocular visual functions.

- **Fixation** is the act of making visual contact with a target and is largely a conscious eye movement. During a fixation the eye receives information via the retina from the environment and after preprocessing this information, delivers it to the brain.

- **Saccades** are rapid eye movements essential for visual tracking or scanning of images like small print. Its angular velocity depends on amplitudes, ranging from 60 to a maximum of 600 degrees per second. During a saccade, the eyes do not receive any visual information and we are indeed blind for a few milliseconds due to suppression. During these phases of perception suppression, data most recently received are presumably still being processed.

- **Pursuits** are the type of eye movements used when following a moving target such as a ball.

- **Intermittent central suppression (ICS)** is a deletion of details of visual perception lasting only for milliseconds. This deletion of perceptions occurs in the center of the retina (on / off phenomenon) and only in binocular vision. This perception disorder has nothing to do with the deep and long-lasting suppression of the perceptions of a squinting eye and the resulting weakness of vision (amblyopia). Rather, the neurophysiology of ICS belongs in the same category as a short-term image deletion during a very rapid gaze under monocular vision. However, ICS lasts longer and can severely impair the ability to read.

- **Visuomotor coordination** is the adjustment of eye movements in conjunction with body and hand movements, also called eye-hand coordination.

- **Figure-ground perception** is the visual ability to distinguish and recognize shapes and objects from a visually structured background.

- **Perception of spatial orientation** is the visual ability to recognize the spatial position and relationships between shapes and objects in relation to our own position in space.

- **Perception of form constancy** is the visual ability to recognize forms and objects as the same regardless of size, color, or angle of view.

- **Perception of visual orientation** is the visual ability to assess tilt angles in lines, length, and distances.

Made in the USA
Middletown, DE
01 October 2017